The Peeragogy Handbook

with contributions from
Bryan Alexander, Paul Allison, Régis Barondeau,
Doug Breitbart, George Brett, Suz Burroughs,
Joseph Corneli, Jay Cross, Charles Jeffrey Danoff,
Julian Elve, María Fernanda, James Folkestad,
Kathy Gill, John Graves, Gigi Johnson,
Anna Keune, Kyle Larson, Roland Legrand,
Amanda Lyons, Christopher Neal, Ted Newcomb,
Stephanie Parker, Charlotte Pierce, David Preston,
Howard Rheingold, Paola Ricaurte, Stephanie Schipper,
Fabrizio Terzi, and Geoff Walker

Tuesday 5th November, 2013 (version 1.3)

All the text in this book has been donated to the
Public Domain.

SMALL CAPS corresponds to links in the online version
of the book, which is at HTTP://PEERAGOGY.ORG.

CONTENTS

I	INTRODUCTION	1
1	WELCOME!	3
2	HOW TO USE THIS HANDBOOK	5
II	PEER LEARNING	7
3	AN OVERVIEW	9
III	MOTIVATION	29
4	WHY WE'RE DOING THIS	31
5	CASE STUDY: 5PH1NX	37
IV	PEERAGOGY IN PRACTICE	57
6	THINKING ABOUT PATTERNS	59
7	PATTERNS AND HEURISTICS	67
8	PATTERNS	71
9	ANTIPATTERNS	83
V	CONVENING A GROUP	91
10	CONVENING	93
11	PLAY AND LEARNING	101
12	K-12 PEERAGOGY	105
VI	ORGANIZING A LEARNING CONTEXT	113
13	ORGANIZING CO-LEARNING	115
14	ADDING STRUCTURE	125

15	The student authored syllabus	131
16	How to Organize a MOOC	139
17	Participation	149
18	The Workscape	153

VII Cooperation — 157
19	Co-facilitation	159
20	Designs for co-working	167
21	Platform design	173

VIII Assessment — 179
22	Peeragogical Assessment	181
23	Following the money	187
24	Researching Peeragogy	189

IX Technologies, Services, and Platforms — 197
25	Peeragogy Technology	199
26	Forums	211
27	Wiki	217
28	Real-time Meetings	225

X Resources — 231
29	How to get involved	233
30	Peeragogy in Action	237
31	Style Guide	245
32	Meet the Authors	249

Part I

Introduction

CHAPTER 1

WELCOME TO THE PEERAGOGY HANDBOOK

Welcome to the Peeragogy Handbook!
Peeragogy is a collection of techniques for collaborative learning and collaborative work. By learning how to "work smart" together, we hope to leave the world in a better state than it was when we arrived.

Indeed, humans have always learned from each other. But for a long time – until the advent of the Web and widespread access to digital media – schools have had an effective monopoly on the business of learning. Now, with access to open educational resources and free or inexpensive communication platforms, groups of people can learn together outside as well as inside formal institutions. All of this prompted us to reconsider the meaning of "peer learning."

The *Peeragogy Handbook* isn't a normal book; it is an example of the kind of work that's only just now possible. The book is an evolving guide, and it tells a collaboratively written story. In fact, it's one that *you* can help write. Using this book, you will develop new norms for the groups you work with — whether online, offline, or both. Every section includes exercises and research methods that you can apply to build and sustain strong and exciting collaborations. When you read the book, you will get to know the authors and will see how we have applied these ideas: in classrooms, in research, in business, and more.

You'll meet Julian, who put the ideas to work as one of the directors of a housing association; Roland, a professional journalist and change-maker; Charlie, a language teacher and writer who works with experimental media for fun and profit; and Charlotte, an indie publisher who wants to become better at what she does by helping others learn how to do it well too — as well as many other contributors from around the world.

The book focuses on techniques for BUILDING A STRONG

Welcome!

GROUP, ORGANIZING A LEARNING SPACE, DOING COOPERATIVE WORK, and CONDUCTING EFFECTIVE PEER ASSESSMENT. These major sections are complemented by a catalog of design patterns and notes on relevant technologies. You should, for this reason, think of the book as first and foremost a practical guide. As you work through these chapters, you will begin mastering these techniques and developing the way you think about getting things done.

The following brief section is a guide to using the book itself. Then, we provide a succinct overview of the book's contents which will help you begin thinking like a peeragogue. Once again, future editions CAN INCLUDE YOUR VOICE, so don't hesitate to GET IN TOUCH with comments or questions.

CHAPTER 2

HOW TO USE THIS HANDBOOK

Author: Howard Rheingold This document is a practical guide to co-learning, a living document that invites comment and invites readers to join the community of editors; the document does not have to be read in linear order from beginning to end.

If you and a group of other people want to co-learn together, this handbook is a practical tool for learning how to self-organize peer learning – what we call "peeragogy." Material about conceptualizing and convening co-learning – the stuff about getting started – is located toward the top of the table of contents. Material about assessment, resources, use cases is located toward the bottom of the TOC. But you don't have to read it in sequential order. Hop around if you'd like. We've focused on "hands-on" techniques, so you'll probably want to try things out with your own groups and networks. We think – and some research seems to support – that understanding how co-learning works will help you do co-learning more effectively. So we've included material about learning theories that support peer learning or that reveal useful characteristics of successful peer learning. For those who want to delve more deeply into the empirical research and scholarship, we've linked to a sister document – a literature review of learning theory related to peeragogy. For those who want to study more deeply about the aspects of peer learning we summarize in our articles, we provide a list of links to related handbook articles, and a set of resources for further study. Think of our pages as both places to start and as jumping off points.

The short videos, most of them under one minute long, at the very beginning of many articles are meant to convey a sense of what the article and its supporting material is meant to convey.

This is a living document. If you want to join our community of editors, contact HOWARD@RHEINGOLD.COM. If you want to know more about how to go about creating a handbook entry,

How to use this handbook

see the guides at the end of this book. If you don't want to go as far submitting new articles or editing existing ones, please feel free to use the comment thread attached to each page to suggest changes and/or additions.

See also

- G‍uide to getting started
- T‍he Table of Contents
- O‍ur list of resources
- O‍ur literature review

Part II

Peer Learning

CHAPTER 3

AN OVERVIEW OF PEER LEARNING

The aim of the *Peeragogy Handbook* is to establish effective peer-learning techniques that you can implement "on the ground." We suggest that you look through the Handbook, try a few of these suggestions, and see how they work for you. Then we invite you to return here, share your experiences, ask for feedback, and work with us to improve the Handbook and the field we affectionately call "Peeragogy."

In this part of the *Peeragogy Handbook*, teams of "peeragogues" have distilled their most important and applicable research and insights from more than a year of inquiry and discussion. Although there's been no shortage of experimentation and formal research into collaborative, connective, and shared learning systems in the past, we've detected a new rumbling among education thinkers that when combined with new platforms and technologies, peer-learning strategies as described here could have a huge impact on the way educational institutions evolve in the future. We've also seen for ourselves how peer-learning techniques can help anyone who's interested become an effective informal educator, whether or not that's part of their job description.

The interplay of individual and group

"Personal" supports "peer" - We can consciously cultivate living, growing, responsive webs of information, support, and inspiration that help us be more effective learners. This is a personal learning network. We'll offer tips on how to build these networks

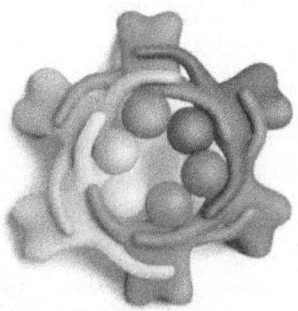

— and we'll also explain how strong personal learning networks can contribute to and evolve into even stronger peer learning networks.

"Peer" supports "personal" - As we work together to develop shared plans for our collective efforts in group projects, we usually can find places where we have something to learn. Furthermore, if we are willing to ask for help and offer our help to others, everybody's learning escalates. Being mindful of effective interpersonal learning patterns is an important part of building an effective personal learning plan.

In the following sections, you can read some more about these strategies, or you can skip ahead to Part III to start looking at specific techniques you can use to build your own peer learning group.

Peer learning through the ages

As you may have guessed, our new term, peeragogy, is a riff on the word pedagogy — the art, science, or profession of teaching. Pedagogy has a somewhat problematic story of origin: it comes from the ancient Greek tradition of having a child (paidos) be supervised (agogos) by a slave. Greek philosophers disagreed with each other as to the best way for individuals to gain knowledge (and even more so, wisdom). Socrates, who insisted that he was not wise, also insisted that his interlocutors join him in investigating truth claims, as peers. The most famous of these interlocutors, Plato, on a more pedagogical bent, spoke of an enlightened few, whose responsibility it was to show others the light of knowledge (illustrated by his famous allegory of "The Cave").

In more recent centuries, various education theorists and reformers have challenged the effectiveness of what had become the traditional teacher-led model. Most famous of the early education reformers in the United States was John Dewey, who advocated new experiential learning techniques. In his 1916 book, *Democracy and Education* [1], Dewey wrote, "Education is not an affair of 'telling' and being told, but an active and constructive process." Soviet psychologist Lev Vygotsky, who developed the concept of the Zone of Proximal Development, was another proponent of "constructivist" learning. His book, *Thought and Language*, also gives evidence to support collaborative, socially meaningful, problem-solving activities over isolated exercises.

Within the last few decades, things have begun to change very rapidly. In "Connectivism: A Learning Theory for the Digital Age," George Siemens argues that technology has changed the way we learn, explaining how it tends to complicate or expose the limitations of the learning theories of the past [3]. The crucial point of connectivism is that the connections that make it possible for us to learn in the future are more relevant than the sets of knowledge we know individually in the present. Furthermore, technology can, to some degree and in certain contexts, replace know-how with know-where-to-look.

If you want more details on the history, theories, and recent experiments related to peer learning, we have a more extensive literature review available. We've also adapted it into a Wikipedia page, which you can edit as well as read.

From peer learning to peeragogy

The idea that we needed a new theory (which we gave the name "paragogy" [4]) arose out of the challenges we faced doing peer learning. Our aim was to understand how groups and organizations can become better at serving participants' interests, while participants also learn and become better contributors.

An Overview

PLATON CAVE SANRAEDAM (1604). By Jan Saenredam [Public domain], via Wikimedia Commons

Paragogy began as a set of proposed principles that describe peer produced peer learning – we'll say exactly what these principles are a bit further below. We designed them to contrast with a set guidelines for adult educators advanced by Malcolm Knowles [5]. The paragogy principles focused on the way in which co-learners shape their learning context together. Peer produced peer learning is something for "innovative educators" everywhere, working at all scales. You don't need to have the word teacher, trainer, or educator in your job title. It's enough to invite someone out to lunch and ask questions, set up a reading group with your friends, or even to tackle a new DIY project following tips from the hardware store clerk or instructions you downloaded from the internet.

Our secret for successful peer learning is actually hidden in plain view: the word "paragogy" means "production" in Greek. We're particularly interested in how the powerful blend of peer learning and collaborative work drives open source software development, and helps build resources like Wikipedia. But in fact it works equally well in offline settings, from official hacker/maker

An Overview

spaces to garages and treehouses. Projects like STORYCORPS show how contemporary media can add a powerful new layer to ancient strategies for teaching, learning, and sharing.

The word "peeragogy" attempts to make these ideas immediately understandable to everyone, including non-geeks. Peeragogy is about peers learning together, and teaching each other. In the end, the two words are actually synonyms. If you want to go into theory-building mode, you can spell it "paragogy". If you want to be a bit more down to earth, stick with "peeragogy."

References

1. Dewey, J. (2004). Democracy and education. Dover Publications.

2. Vygotsky, L. S. (1986). Thought and language. MIT press.

3. Siemens, G. (2005). Connectivism: A learning theory for the digital age. International Journal of Instructional Technology and Distance Learning, 2(1), 3-10.

4. Corneli, J. and Danoff, C.J. (2011), Paragogy: Synergizing individual and organizational learning. (Published on Wikiversity.)

5. Knowles, M. S. (1980). The modern practice of adult education: From pedagogy to andragogy. Chicago: Follett.

Which is more fun, skateboarding or physics?

An introduction to the patterns associated with peer learning. Consider the following learning scenarios:

1. A study group for a tough class in Honors Physics convenes at at the library late one night, resolving to do well on the next day's exam. The students manage to deflect their

purpose for a while by gossiping about hook-ups and parties, studying for other classes, and sharing photos. Then, first one member, then another, takes the initiative and as a group, the students eventually pull their attention back to the task at hand. They endure the monotony of studying for several hours, and the next day, they own the exam.

2. A young skateboarder spends hours tweaking the mechanics of how to make a skateboard float in the air for a split second, enduring physical pain of repeated wipeouts. With repetition and success comes a deep understanding of the physics of the trick. That same student cannot string together more than five minutes of continuous attention during class and spends even less time on homework for the class before giving up.

Peer-learning participants succeed when they are motivated to learn. Skateboarding is primarily intrinsically motivated, with some extrinsic motivation coming from the respect that kids receive from peers when they master a trick. In most cases, the primary motivation for learning physics is extrinsic, coming from parents' and society's expectations that the student excel and assure his or her future by getting into a top college.

The student very well could be intrinsically motivated to have a glowing report card, but not for the joy of learning physics, but because of the motivation to earn a high grade as part of her overall portfolio. Taken a different way, what is it about physics that's fun for a student who does love the science? Perhaps she anticipates the respect, power and prestige that comes from announcing a new breakthrough; or she may feel her work is important for the greater good, or prosperity, of humanity; or she may simply be thrilled to see atoms bonding to form new compounds.

Learning situations frequently bore the learner when extrinsic motivation is involved. Whether by parents or society, being forced to do something, as opposed to choosing to, ends up making the individual less likely to succeed. In some cases it's clear, but trying to figure out what makes learning fun for a group of in-

An Overview

Photo of Dmitri Mendeleev (1834-1907). Found on The Guardian's Notes & Theories blog. Public domain.

dividual humans can be very difficult. Often there is no clear-cut answer that can be directly applied in the learning environment. Either way, identifying the factors that can make learning boring or fun is a good start. Perhaps learning certain skills or topics is intrinsically boring, no matter what, and we have to accept that.

Learning patterns

One way to think about fun learning is that it's fun to learn - and be aware that you're learning - new patterns. Jürgen Schmidhuber wrote: "A [...] learner maximizes expected fun by finding or creating data that is better compressible in some yet unknown but learnable way, such as jokes, songs, paintings, or scientific observations obeying novel, unpublished laws" [1]. So the skateboarder enjoyed coming across new patterns: novel tricks that were nonetheless learnable.

Learner, know thyself: a self-evaluation technique

The learning contributed and acquired by each member of the peer learning enterprise depends on a healthy sense of self-awareness. When you ask yourself, "What do I have to offer?" and "What do I get out of it?" we think you'll come up with some exciting answers. In peer learning, whether or not you're pursuing a practical objective, you're in charge, and this kind of learning is usually fun. Indeed, as we'll describe below, there are deep links between play and learning. We believe we can improve the co-learning experience by adopting a playful mindset. Certainly some of our best learning moments in the Peeragogy project have been peppered with humor and banter. So we found that a key strategy for successful peer learning is to engage in a self-assessment of your motivations and abilities. In this exercise, you take into account factors like the learning context, timing and sequence of learning activities, social reinforcements, and visible reward. The peeragogical view is that learning is most effective when it contains some form of enjoyment or satisfaction, or when it leads to a concrete accomplishment.

When joining the Peeragogy project, Charles Jeffrey Danoff did a brief self-evaluation about what makes him interested in learning:

1. **Context.** I resist being groomed for some unforeseeable future rather than for a specific purpose.

2. **Timing and sequence.** I find learning fun when I'm studying something as a way to procrastinate on another pressing assignment.

3. **Social reinforcement.** Getting tips from peers on how to navigate a snowboard around moguls was more fun for me than my Dad showing me the proper way to buff the car's leather seats on chore day.

4. **Experiential awareness.** In high school, it was not fun to sit and compose a 30-page reading journal for Frankenstein.

An Overview

But owing in part to those types of prior experiences, I now find writing pleasurable and it's fun to learn how to write better.

We will explore the patterns of peer learning in more detail in the section on PRACTICE.

Reference

1. Schmidhuber, J. (2010). Formal theory of creativity, fun, and intrinsic motivation. Autonomous Mental Development (IEEE), 2(3), 230-247.

What kind of help do you need?

An introduction to convening a great peer learning group

Personal Learning Networks and Peer Learning Networks

Personal Learning Networks are the collections of people and information resources (and relationships with them) that people cultivate in order to form their own public or private learning networks — living, growing, responsive sources of information, support, and inspiration that support self-learners.

Howard Rheingold: "When I started using social media in the classroom, I looked for and began to learn from more experienced educators. First, I read and then tried to comment usefully on their blog posts and tweets. When I began to understand who knew what in the world of social media in education, I narrowed my focus to the most knowledgeable and adventurous among them. I paid attention to the

An Overview

people the savviest social media educators paid attention to. I added and subtracted voices from my attention network, listened and followed, then commented and opened conversations. When I found something I thought would interest the friends and strangers I was learning from, I passed along my own learning through my blogs and Twitter stream. I asked questions, asked for help, and eventually started providing answers and assistance to those who seemed to know less than I. The teachers I had been learning from had a name for what I was doing — "growing a personal learning network." So I started looking for and learning from people who talked about HOW to grow a "PLN" as the enthusiasts called them.

Strong and weak ties

Your PLN will have people and sites that you check on often – your main sources of information and learning – your 'strong ties'. Your 'weak ties' are those people and sites that you don't allow a lot of bandwidth or time. But they may become strong later, as your network grows or your interests expand. This is a two-way street – it is very important that you are sharing what you learn and discover with those in your network and not just taking, if you want to see your network expand.

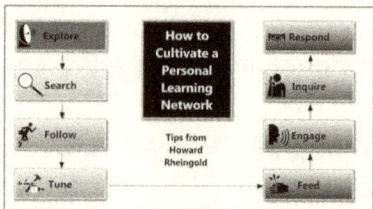

Peer learning networks

In the section on "CONVENING A GROUP", we'll talk about how to develop and share "peeragogical profiles" — how to advertise what you want to learn, and what you'd be interested in helping teach others, and how to use this to build effective connections. You'll also find more information about building a peer learning network in our article on Peeragogy for K-12 Educators (the article is useful even if you're not formally employed as a teacher).

How should we structure things?

An introduction to organizing peer learning experiences

From syllabus and curriculum to personal and peer learning plans

Part of the effectiveness of peeragogy is that the "syllabus" or "curriculum" – more generally, the learning plan – is developed by the people doing the learning. You don't faint with shock when you see the reading list if you helped write it.

In peer learning, having a personal learning plan at the outset helps each participant identify his or her unique learning and teaching proclivities and capabilities, and effectively apply them in the peer setting. In developing your personal plan, you can ask yourself the following questions:

1. What do I most need to learn about in the time ahead?

2. What are the best ways I learn, what learning activities will meet my learning needs, what help will I need and how long will it take?

3. What will I put into my personal portfolio to demonstrate my learning progress and achievements?

Early in the process, the peer-learning group should also convene to develop a peer learning plan. In the Peeragogy project, we used live meetings and forum-style platforms to discuss the group-level versions of the questions listed above. Personal learning needs and skills were also aired via these platforms, but the key shared outcome was an initial project plan. Initially this took the form of an outline of handbook chapters to write, as well as a division of labor into different roles.

Nothing was set in stone, and both the peer group and individual participants have continued to develop, implement, review, and adjust their goals as the project develops. We have stayed sufficiently connected to the original goal of producing a handbook about peer learning that you now have one in your hands (or on your screen). We've also added some new goals for the project as time has gone by.

Having a malleable framework enables peer learners to:

1. Identify appropriate directions and goals for future learning;

2. Review their strengths and areas for development;

3. Identify goals and plans for improvement;

4. Monitor their actions and review and adjust plans as needed to achieve their goals;

5. Update the goals to correspond to progress.

This doesn't mean you have to let chaos rule, but often in the swirl of ideas and contributions, new directions took shape and new ideas took hold. We expand on the notion of change in the discussion of roles and motivations.

Self-generating templates

Documentation like mind maps, outlines, blogs or journals, and forum posts for a peer learning project can create an "audit trail," or history, of the process. This record not only serves as a guide for new participants, but also functions as a valuable review tool for all, and a ready-made template for future peer-learning projects. As you mine the documentation of a past peer-learning project or a completed phase of an ongoing project for

An Overview

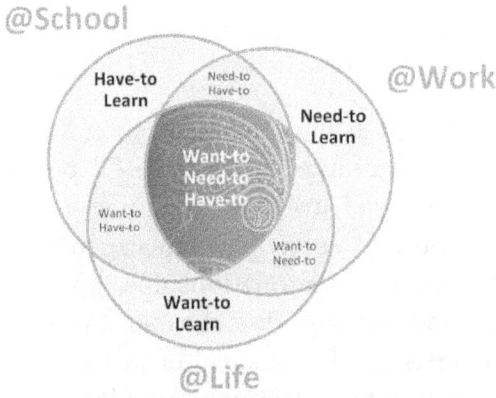

"I think because of the tremendous changes we see in education and at work, the sets (attitudes) are beginning to overlap more and more," said Joachim Stroh of the Google+ community, Visual Metaphors.

effective learning patterns, take the time to validate and compare what you've achieved against the goal or mission at the outset. Use the record to reflect and evaluate key elements of the process for you as a facilitator and as a member of the peer learning group. Update your plans accordingly.

From corporate training to learning on the job

Today's knowledge workers typically have instant, ubiquitous access to the internet. The measure of their ability is an open-book exam. "What do you know?" is replaced with "What can you do?" And if they get bored, they can relatively easily be mentally elsewhere.

This has ramifications for the way managers manage as well as the way teachers teach. To extract optimal performance from workers, managers must inspire them rather than command them. Antoine de Saint-Exupéry put it nicely: "If you want to build a boat, do not instruct the men to saw wood, stitch the sails, prepare the tools and organize the work, but make them long for setting sail and travel to distant lands."

> **Jay Cross**: "If I were an instructional designer in a moribund training department, I'd polish up my resume and head over to marketing. Co-learning can differentiate services, increase product usage, strengthen customer relationships, and reduce the cost of hand-holding. It's cheaper and more useful than advertising. But instead of just making a copy of today's boring educational practices, build something based on interaction and camaraderie, perhaps with some healthy competition thrown in. Again, the emphasis should always be on learning in order to do something!"

In the section on ORGANIZING A LEARNING CONTEXT, we'll say quite a bit more about the implications that our full conception of peer learning has for managers, teachers, and other facilitators.

Can we work together on this?

An introduction to "paragogy", the productive side of peer learning.

Metacognition and mindfulness in peer learning

Metacognition and mindfulness have to do with your awareness how how you think, talk, participate, and attend to circumstances. It can be particularly useful to apply this sort of "meta awareness" as you think about the roles that you take on in a given project, the kind of contributions you want to make, and what you hope to get out of the experience. These are all likely to change as time, so it's good to get in the habit of reflection.

Potential roles in your peer-learning project

1. Leader, Manager, Team Member, Worker

2. Content Creator, Author, Content Processor, Reviewer, Editor

3. Presentation Creator, Designer, Graphics, Applications

4. Planner, Project Manager, Coordinator, Attendee, Participant

5. Mediator, Moderator, Facilitator, Proponent, Advocate, Representative, Contributor

Potential contributions

1. Create, Originate, Research, Aggregate

2. Develop, Design, Integrate, Refine, Convert

3. Write, Edit, Layout

Potential motivations

1. Acquisition of training or support in a topic or field;

2. Building relationships with interesting people;

3. Finding professional opportunities through other participants;

4. Creating or bolstering a personal network;

5. More organized and rational thinking through dialog and debate;

6. Feedback about performance and understanding of the topic.

An Overview

A famous work in ink by Sengai Gibon (1750–1837)

The process of shared reflection can prime a group for cohesion and success. It can be tremendously useful to think about the motivations of other participants, and how these can be jointly served. How can we re-use the "side-effects" of individual and cooperative efforts in a useful way?

Two theories of motivation

One of the most prominent current thinkers of (self-)motivation and regulation is Daniel Pink [1], who proposes a theory of motivation based on autonomy, mastery, and purpose, or, more colorfully:

1. The urge to direct my life

2. The desire to get better at something that matters

3. The yearning to do something that serves a purpose bigger than just "myself"

There's clearly a "learning orientation" behind the second point: in fact, it's not just a matter of "fun" — ultimately, it's the sense of achievement that matters.

Learning is given an even more central position in a paper by Thomas Malone [2], who was another thinker who asked "What makes things fun to learn?". His proposed framework for motivating learning activities is based on the three ingredients fantasy, challenge, and curiosity — this bears a certain analogy to Pink's framework.

We can easily see how "participation" relates to "motivation" in the sense described here. When I get useful information from other people, I can direct my own life better. When I have means of exploring my fantasies and dreams by chatting then over and exploring some of the elements in a safe way, I'm in a much better position to make something in reality. A solid reputation that comes from being able to help others serves as a good indicator of personal progress, and a sign that one is able to deal with greater challenges. Relationships provide the most basic sense of being part of something bigger than just oneself: et cetera. Further thoughts on the role of motivation in peer learning appear in our chapter on our Motivation for working on this book. And we'll say more about various features of productive co-working in the section on COOPERATION.

References

1. Pink, D. (2011), Drive: The Surprising Truth About What Motivates Us, Canongate Books Ltd

2. Malone, T.W. (1981), Toward a Theory of Intrinsically Motivating Instruction, Cognitive Science, 4, pp. 333-369

How do we know if we've won?

An introduction to peeragogical asssessment

Different ways to analyze the learning process

After doing some personal reflection on the roles you want to take on and the contributions you want to make (as we discussed above), you may also want to work together with your learning group to analyze the learning process in more detail. There are many different phases, stages, and dimensions that you can use to help structure and understand the learning experience: we list some of these below.

1. I, We, Its, It (from Ken Wilber – for an application in modeling educational systems, see [1])

2. Guidance & Support, Communication & Collaboration, Reflection & Demonstration, Content & Activities (from Gráinne Conole)

3. Forming, Norming, Storming, Performing from Bruce Tuckman.

4. The "five-stage e-moderating model" from Gilly Salmon

5. Assimilative, Information Processing, Communicative, Productive, Experiential, Adaptive (from Oliver and Conole)

6. Multiple intelligences (after Howard Gardner).

7. The associated "mental state" (after Csíkszentmihályi; see picture)

8. Considered in terms of "Learning Power" (Deakin-Crick, Broadfoot, and Claxton).

Peer learning for one

How can you apply the ideas of peer learning on your own? In a certain sense, it's impossible, but somehow that never stops people from trying. We find a striking parallel between the paragogy principles and the 5 Elements of Effective Thinking proposed by Edward Burger and Michael Starbird in a recent book [2]. It's a nice short book and worth a read: here, we will just quote the titles of the main chapters to illustrate one possible parallel:

An Overview

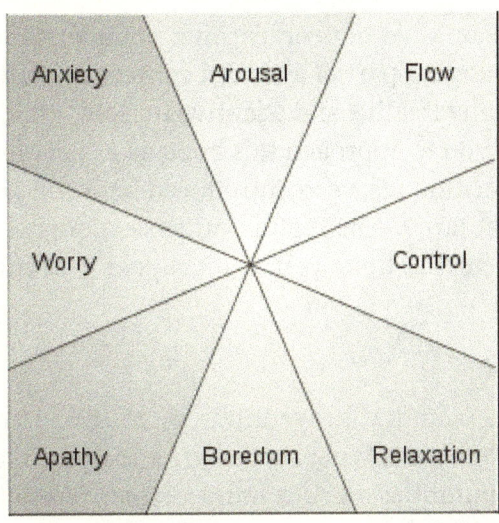

CHALLENGE VS. SKILL. By w:User:Oliverbeatson (w:File:Challenge vs skill.jpg) [Public domain]

1. Changing context as a decentered center ~ Quintessence, Engaging Change: Transform Yourself

2. Meta-learning as a font of knowledge ~ Earth, Grounding Your Thinking: Understanding Deeply

3. Peers provide feedback that wouldn't be there otherwise ~ Air, Creating Questions out of Thin Air: Be your own Socrates

4. Learning is distributed and nonlinear ~ Water, Seeing the Flow of Ideas: Look Back, Look Forward

5. Realize the dream if you can, then wake up! ~ Fire, Igniting Insights through Mistakes: Fail to Succeed

We think that "thinking" is often most effective when it's done with others, and this is something that Burger and Starbird don't give much attention. Nevertheless, even when you find yourself on your own in the midst of that challenging DIY project, you can use the techniques of peer learning to understand yourself as a growing, changing part of a shared context in motion. This can contribute to an effective and adaptive outlook on life.

We invite you to approach this book as a "peer learner" – and we hope the techniques we've introduced here will serve you well in the world at large. The section on PEERAGOGICAL ASSESSMENT will help you further hone your critical peer learning edge.

References

1. Corneli, J., and Mikroyannidis, A. (2012). Crowdsourcing education on the Web: a role-based analysis of online learning communities, in Alexandra Okada, Teresa Conolly, and Peter Scott (eds.), Collaborative Learning 2.0: Open Educational Resources, IGI Global.

2. Burger, E. and Starbird, M. (2013). The 5 Elements of Effective Thinking, Princeton University Press.

Part III

Motivation

CHAPTER 4

WHY WE'RE DOING THIS

Participants must bring self-knowledge and no small measure of honesty to the peer-learning project in order to accurately enunciate their motivations. If everyone in your peer learning project asks "What brings me here?" "How can I contribute?" and "How can I contribute more effectively?" things will really start percolating. Test this suggestion by asking these questions of yourself and taking action on the answers!

The primary motivators reported by participants in the Peeragogy project include:

1. Acquisition of training or support in a topic or field;
2. Building relationships with interesting people;
3. Finding professional opportunities through other participants;
4. Creating or bolstering a personal network;
5. More organized and rational thinking through dialog and debate;
6. Feedback about their own performance and understanding of the topic.

Each of those motivators can affect the vitality of the peeragogical process and the end result for the individual participant.

The various motivations also carry some associated risks. For example, if one learner's motivation includes a desire to make business contacts, he or she may be reluctant to share this with the facilitator and other learners for fear of seeming greedy or commercial. Whether or not potential peeragogues eventually decide to assume these risks depends on various factors.

Cultural or societal factors can also complicate motivations and relationships in the peer-learning environment. Actions that typify inappropriate behavior in one culture might represent desirable behavior in another. In the case of culture, motivations can often come out of the closet through conflict; for example, when one learner feels offended or embarrassed by the actions of another.

> **Philip Spalding**: *"The idea of visiting a garden together in a group to learn the names of flowers might have been the original intention for forming a Garden Group. The social aspect of having a day out might be goal of the people participating."*

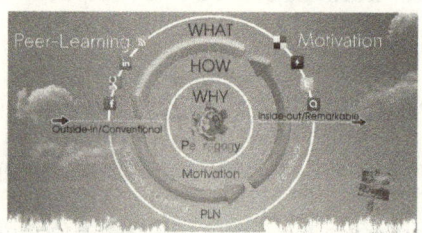

"What's my motivation?"

Example: Peeragogy editor Charlotte Pierce

Basically, I'm here because as an early adopter and admitted gadget freak, I find it fun and rewarding to explore new technologies and topics that I feel have a practical or exciting application. But I have some some other motivations that subtly co-exist alongside my eagerness to explore and learn.

Howard Rheingold's reputation as an innovator and internet pioneer got my attention when he announced his Think-Know

Tools course on Facebook in 2012. I had known of Howard from the 1990's when I was a member of The WELL (Whole Earth 'Lectronic Link). I was curious to see what Howard was up to, so I signed onto the wiki site, paid my $300, and took the course starting in October.

Looking back, I realize we were practicing Peeragogy throughout the TKT course, though at the time I hardly knew peer learning from a pickle. In late November, missing the camaraderie and challenge of TKT, I stepped over to check out The Peeragogy Handbook.

Which brings me to motivations in signing on to Peeragogy. Since Howard and several Think-Know Tools co-learners were already dedicating their time there and their work looked innovative and exciting, I suspected they might be onto something that I wanted to be a part of. Plus, my brain was primed by the TKT experience. "What if a diverse group of people could learn a subject with little or no cost and not a lot of barriers to entry," I thought. "What if their own experience qualified them to join, contribute, and learn."

I also thought there might be a chance to meet some potential business partners or clients there - but if not, the experience looked rewarding and fun enough for me to take the risk of no direct remuneration. There was no cost to me, and a wealth of knowledge to gain - and a way to be part of something new and exciting. These are always big draws for me. I wanted to be in on it, and nobody was telling me I couldn't!

My projections proved correct. The participants already on board were gracious in welcoming me to Peeragogy, patient in getting me up to speed, and persistent in coaxing me into using the tools central to the project. I connected, learned, grew, and contributed. Now I'm on the brink of starting a peer learning project of my own in my publishing organization, IPNE.org. Stay tuned!

Example: Cafes, schools, workshops

Suppose we wanted to make Peeragogy into a model that can be used in schools, libraries, and so forth, worldwide - and, in fact we do! How can we bring the basic Peeragogy motivations to bear, and make a resource, plan of action, and process that other people can connect with? In brief, how do we build peer learning into the curriculum?

> **Charlotte Pierce:** *With success, these could possibly raise awareness while utilizing the existing framework and population of standard education. A curriculum "unit" using peeragogy, for example, or a seminar in a professional development retreat for teachers. It's not optimum, but it provides an insight from the safety of the existing structure.*

One concrete way to implement these broad aims would be to make a peeragogy-oriented *development* project whose goal is to set up a system of internet cafes, schools, or workshops in places like China or Africa, where people could go to collaborate on work or to learn technical subjects. Students could learn on the job. It seems reasonable to think that investors could make a reasonable profit through "franchises," hardware sales, and so forth – obviously making money is a motivation that a lot of people can connect with.

In developing such a project, we would want to learn from other similar projects that already exist. For example, in Chicago, State Farm Insurance has created a space called the "NEXT DOOR CAFE" that runs community events. One of their offerings is free financial coaching, with the explicit agreement that the issues you discuss return to State Farm as market research.

"Free? Really. Yes, because we're experimenting. We want to learn what people really want. Then, we'll shoot those wants back to the Farm. We help you. You help us innovate. We're all smarter for it. We think it's a win-win." –STATE FARM

Thus, Next Door Cafe forms part of a system to exploit the side-effects of interpersonal interactions to create a system that learns.

A peer learning example from the opposite side of the world started in a slum next to New Delhi where Sugata Mitra gave children a computer and they self organized into a learning community and taught themselves how to use the machine and much more.

> **Sugata Mitra**: I think what we need to look at is we need to look at learning as the product of educational self-organization. If you allow the educational process to self-organize, then learning emerges. It's not about making learning happen. It's about letting it happen.

Reference

1. Hugo Mercier and Dan Sperber, Why do humans reason? Arguments for an argumentative theory, *Behavioral and Brain Sciences* (2011), 34, 57-111

Recommended reading

1. Simon Sinek, *Start With Why: How Great Leaders Inspire Everyone To Take Action*, Penguin Books, 2011

Recommended viewing

1. Sugata Mitra's 2013 TED TALK.

CHAPTER 5

CASE STUDY: 5PH1NX

5PH1NX: 5tudent Peer Heuristic for 1Nformation Xchange - we think of it as a "curiously trans-media" use case in peeragogical assessment.

Author: David Preston, Ph.D.

Over the last several decades technology has driven massive shifts in the way we communicate and collaborate. Information technology, socioeconomic trends, an increasingly complex and uncertain future, and school's failed brand are contributing factors in an emerging discourse that seeks to align learning with our rapidly changing culture. Open Source Learning and Peeragogy, two emerging theoretical frameworks in this discourse, leverage end-to-end user principles of communication technology to facilitate peers learning together and teaching each other. In both traditional and liminal learning communities, one of the major points of contact between education and societal culture is the purposeful use of assessment.

The processes of giving, receiving, and applying constructive critique makes learners better thinkers, innovators, motivators, collaborators, coworkers, friends, relatives, spouses, teammates, and neighbors. Implementing peer-based assessment can be problematic in schooling institutions where evaluative authority is traditionally conflated with hierarchical authority, and where economic and political influences have focused attention on summative, quantitative, standardized measurement of learning and intelligence.

This is the story of how one learning community is adopting Open Source Learning and Peeragogical principles to decentralize and enrich the assessment process.

Knowledge is acquired when we succeed in fitting a new experience into the system of concepts based upon our old experiences. Understanding comes when we liberate ourselves from the old and so make possible a direct, unmediated contact with the new, the mystery, moment by moment, of our existence. -Aldous Huxley, Knowledge & Understanding (1952)

Enter 5PH1NX

On Monday, April 2, 2011, students in three English classes at a California public high school discovered anomalies in the day's entry on their course blog [3]. The date was wrong and the journal topic was this: In The Principles of Psychology (1890), William James wrote, "The faculty of voluntarily bringing back a wandering attention, over and over again, is the very root of judgment, character and will. No one is compos sui if he have it not. An education which should improve this faculty would be the education par excellence." How have your experiences in this course helped you focus your attention? What do you still need to work on? What elements of the following text (from Haruki Murakami's 1Q84) draw your attention and help you construct meaning?

The driver nodded and took the money. "Would you like a receipt?" "No need. And keep the change." "Thanks very much," he said. "Be careful, it looks windy out there. Don't slip." "I'll be careful," Aomame said. "And also," the driver said, facing the mirror, "please remember: things are not what they seem. "Things are not what they seem, Aomame repeated mentally." What do you mean by that?" she asked with knitted brows. The driver

Case Study: 5PH1NX

chose his words carefully: "It's just that you're about to do something out of the ordinary. Am I right? People do not ordinarily climb down the emergency stairs of the Metropolitan Expressway in the middle of the day– especially women." "I suppose you're right." "Right. And after you do something like that, the everyday look of things might seem to change a little. Things may look *different* to you than they did before. I've had that experience myself. But don't let appearances fool you. There's always only one reality."

Find the jokers.

The jokers were real [4] and hidden (without much intent to conceal) around the classroom and in students' journals. Students found them and asked questions about the letters in blue; the questions went unanswered. Some thought it was just another of their teacher's wild hair ideas. Although they didn't know it yet they were playing the liminal role that Oedipus originated in mythology. Solving the riddle would enable them to usher out an old way of thinking and introduce the new. The old way. An authority figure sets the rules, packages the information for a passive audience, and unilaterally evaluates each learner's performance. In that context, peeragogical assessment might be introduced with a theoretical framework, a rubric, and a lesson plan with input, checks for understanding, and guided practice as a foundation for independent work. The new way. In Open Source Learning the learner pursues a path of inquiry within communities that function as end-to-end user networks. Each individual begins her learning with a question and pursues answers through an interdisciplinary course of study that emphasizes multiple modalities and the five Fs: mental Fitness, physical Fitness, spiritual Fitness, civic Fitness, and technological Fitness. Learners collaborate with mentors and receive feedback from experts, community-based peers, and the public. They are the heroes of learning journeys. Heroes don't respond to syllabi. They respond to calls to adventure. Open Source Learning prepares students for the unforeseen. By the time they met the 5PH1NX students had learned about habits of mind, operating schema, digital culture and community, self-expression, collaboration, free play, autonomy, confidence/trust/risk, and resilience. These ideas had been reinforced through nonfiction articles and literary selections such as Montaigne's Essays, Plato's Allegory of the Cave, Bukowski's Laughing Heart, Shakespeare's Hamlet, Sartre's No Exit and others. The first poem assigned in the course was Bukowsk's "Laughing Heart"?: The Gods will give you chances. Know them. Take them. So it is with knowledge and understanding. Today we are presented with an overwhelming, unprecedented quantity and variety of data in our physical and virtual lives; to cope we must improve the ways we seek, select, curate, analyze, evaluate, and act on information. On the back of each Joker card was a QR code that linked to a blog page with riddles and clues to a search. At this point students realized they were playing a game. A tab on the blog page labeled "The Law"? laid out the rules of engagement:

Case Study: 5PH1NX

This Is The Law.

1. You cannot "obey" or "break" The Law. You can only make good decisions or bad decisions.

2. Good decisions lead to positive outcomes.

3. Bad decisions lead to suffering.

4. Success requires humanity.

5. "For the strength of the Pack is the Wolf, and the strength of the Wolf is the Pack." -Rudyard Kipling

6. "The Way of the sage is to act but not to compete." -Lao Tzu

7. Be honorable.

8. Have fun.

9. Question.

10. Sapere aude.

This is The Law. After a second set of on-campus and blog quests, students noticed a shift in 5PH1NX. A couple of weeks before the first clue was published, during a Socratic seminar on Derrida's concept of Free Play, a student said, "We learn best when adults take away the crutches and there is no safety net." The quote was used in the next clue; students began to realize that the game was not pre-determined. 5PH1NX was evolving in response to their contributions. This is a manifestation of the hackneyed writing cliché: show, don't tell.

Case Study: 5PH1NX

> "We learn best when adults take away the crutches and there is no safety net."
> –Some kid

Welcome. You're here because you're smart, determined, charismatic, persuasive, good-looking, devious, lucky, or some combination of the seven.

5PH1NX is bemused but not yet impressed.

To demonstrate your worthiness, and to accrue a host of other benefits that have not been itemized, described, explained, implied, or promised to you by anyone, complete as many of the following FEATS OF WISDOM® as you can. You must complete a minimum of four FEATS OF WISDOM® in order to be eligible for the following week. If you can complete all of the FEATS OF WISDOM® you will become a liminal figure who will co-author the finale of this experience.

NOTE 1: Lurkers who want to watch the show but keep to the shadows can participate in quests and accrue aforementioned benefits by supporting and documenting others' efforts.

NOTE 2: No post counts unless it includes the image of the 5PH1NX as seen above. You may reproduce this image as many times and in as many ways as you need to.

NOTE 3: The FEATS OF WISDOM® are numbered. For each of the FEATS OF WISDOM® you complete, you will create a blog post. Title each blog post FEATS OF WISDOM® #[ ] and include the correct number of the feat you're documenting in that post.

NOTE 4: Wisdom is recursive. That means going back to the task again and again in order to obtain better results and deepen the experience. So... if you want to repeat one of the FEATS OF WISDOM® , you may, and you may do it as many times as you want to for experience credit (not to mention the LULZ).

FEATS OF WISDOM®

The student's comment was a call to action. The Feats of Wisdom were designed to engage learners over a vacation break in fun, collaborative, social media-friendly missions that required engagement in the community, expansion of their personal learning networks, and documentation on their blogs. For example:

CASE STUDY: 5PH1NX

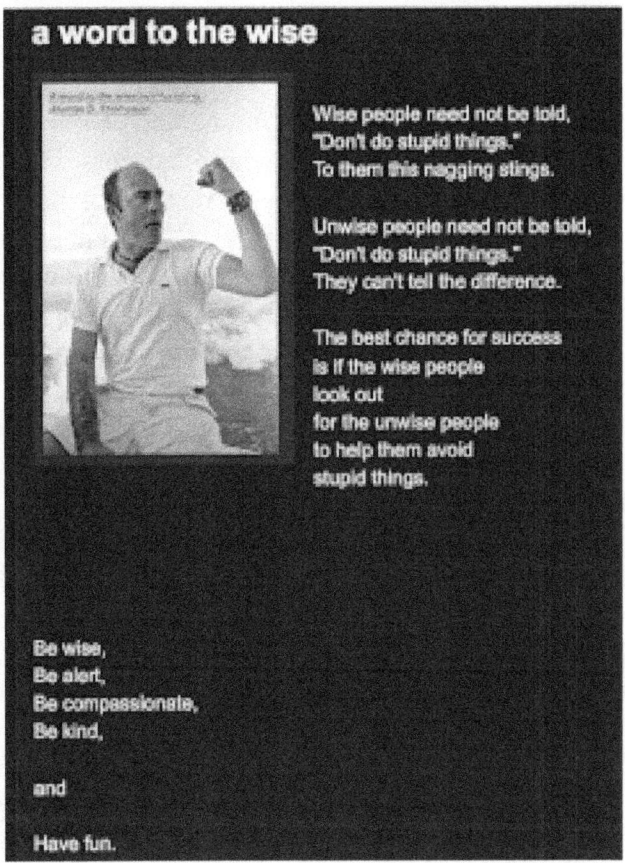

FEAT #1

Buy a ticket to "The Hunger Games" (or any other movie that's likely to draw a large, young, rowdy audience). Before the lights dim and the trailers begin, walk to the screen, turn to the audience, and in a loud, clear voice, recite the "To be, or not to be..." soliloquy from Hamlet (don't worry if you make a couple mistakes, just be sure you make it all the way to, "Be all my sins remembered."). CAPTURE THE EVENT ON VIDEO & POST IT TO YOUR BLOG.

Students had been using the Internet without an Acceptable Use Policy all year; such policies are one-to-many artifacts of a central authority and far weaker than community norms. So rather than introduce "rules" 5PH1NX simply provided a reminder of the client-side responsibility:

Case Study: 5PH1NX

The Emergence of Peeragogical Assessment

The third page on the Feats of Wisdom blog was entitled Identifying and Rewarding Greatness, where learners were greeted with the following paragraph: If you see something that was done with love, that pushed the boundaries, set the standard, broke the mold, pushed the envelope, raised the bar, blew the doors off, or rocked in some previously unspecified way, please bring it to the attention of the tribe by posting a link to it [here].

No one did. Instead, they started doing something more effective. They started building. One student hacked the entire game and then created her own version. Other students began to consider the implications for identifying and rewarding greatness. They realized that one teacher couldn't possibly observe how 96 students were working over vacation out in the community and online to accomplish the Feats of Wisdom.

In order to get credit for their efforts they would have to curate and share their work process and product. They also realized that the same logic applied to learning and coursework in general; after all, even the most engaged, conscientious teacher only sees a high school or college student a few hours a week in artificial conditions. The learner presumably spends her whole life in the company of her own brain. Who is the more qualified reporting authority? With these thoughts in mind students created Project Infinity, a peer-to-peer assessment platform through which students could independently assign value to those thoughts and activities they deemed worthy.

Because the 2011-12 5PH1NX was a three-week exercise in gamification, Project Infinity quickly evolved to include collaborative working groups and coursework. This was learner-centered Peeragogical assessment in action; learners identified a need and an opportunity, they built a tool for the purpose, they managed it themselves, and they leveraged it in a meaningful way to support student achievement in the core curriculum.

Project Infinity 2 & Implications for the Future

Alumni from the Class of 2012 felt such a strong positive connection to their experience in Open Source Learning and Peeragogical assessment that they built a version for the Class of 2013. They created Project Infinity2 with enhanced functionality. They asked the teacher to embed an associated Twitter feed on the course blog, then came to classes to speak with current students about their experiences. Everyone thought the Class of 2013 would stand on the shoulders of giants and adopt the platform with similar enthusiasm. They were wrong. Students understood the concept and politely contributed suggestions for credit, but it quickly became evident that they weren't enthusiastic. Submissions decreased and finally the Project Infinity2 Twitter feed disappeared from the course blog. Learners' blogs and project work (here and here) suggested that they were mastering the core curriculum and meta concepts, and they appeared generally excited about Open Source Learning overall. So why weren't they more excited about the idea of assessing themselves and each other? Because Project Infinity wasn't theirs. They didn't get to build it. It was handed to them in the same way that a syllabus is handed to them. No matter how innovative or effective it might be, Project Infinity was just another tool designed by someone else to get students to do something they weren't sure they wanted/needed to do in the first place. Timing may be a factor. Last year's students didn't meet 5PH1NX until the first week in April, well into the spring semester. This year's cohort started everything faster and met 5PH1NX in November. Now (in January) they understand the true potential of their situation and they're taking the reins. As students realized what was happening with the clues and QR codes they approached the teacher and last year's alumni with a request: Let Us In. They don't just want to design learning materials or creatively demonstrate mastery, they want to chart their own course and build the vehicle/s for taking the trip. Alumni and students are becoming Virtual TAs who will start the formal peer-to-peer advising and grading process. In the Spring Semester all students will be asked to prepare a statement of goals/intentions, and they will be informed that the traditional teacher will be responsible for no more than 30% of their grade. The rest will come from a community of peers, experts and members of the public. On Tuesday of Finals Week 5PH1NX went from five players to two hundred. Sophomores and freshman have jumped into the fray and hacked/solved one of the blog clues before seniors did. Members of the Open Source Learning cohort have also identified opportunities to enrich and expand 5PH1NX. A series of conversations about in-person retreats and the alumni community led to students wanting to create a massively multiple player learning cohort. Imagine 50,000-100,000 learners collaborating and sharing information on a quest to pass an exam "by solving a game that leads them to a "Learning Man Festival"? in the Summer of 2013. When 5PH1NX players return from Winter Break in January they will transform their roles relative to the game and the course. Several have already shared "AHA!" moments in which they discovered ways to share ideas and encourage collaboration and peer assessment. They have identified Virtual Teaching Assistant candidates, who will be coached by alumni, and they have plans to provide peer-based assessment for their online work. They are also now actively engaged in taking more control over the collaboration process itself. On the last day of the semester, a post-finals throwaway day of 30-minute class sessions that administrators put on the calendar to collect Average Daily Attendance money, hardly anyone came to campus. Open Source Learning students were all there. They have separated the experience of learning from the temporal, spatial, and cultural constraints of school. They understand how democracy works: those who participate make the decisions. No one knows how this ends, but the outcome of Peeragogical assessment is not a score; it is learners who demonstrate their thinking progress and mastery through social production and peer-based critique. This community's approach to learning and assessment has prepared its members for a complex and uncertain future by moving them from a world of probability to a world of possibility. As one student put it in a video entitled "We Are Superman," "What we are doing now may seem small, but we are part of something so much bigger than we think. What does this prove? It proves everything; it proves that it's possible."

Background

A world in which work looks like what's described in the (PSFK FUTURE OF WORK REPORT 2013) ... requires a learning environment that looks more like this:

and this:

Case Study: 5PH1NX

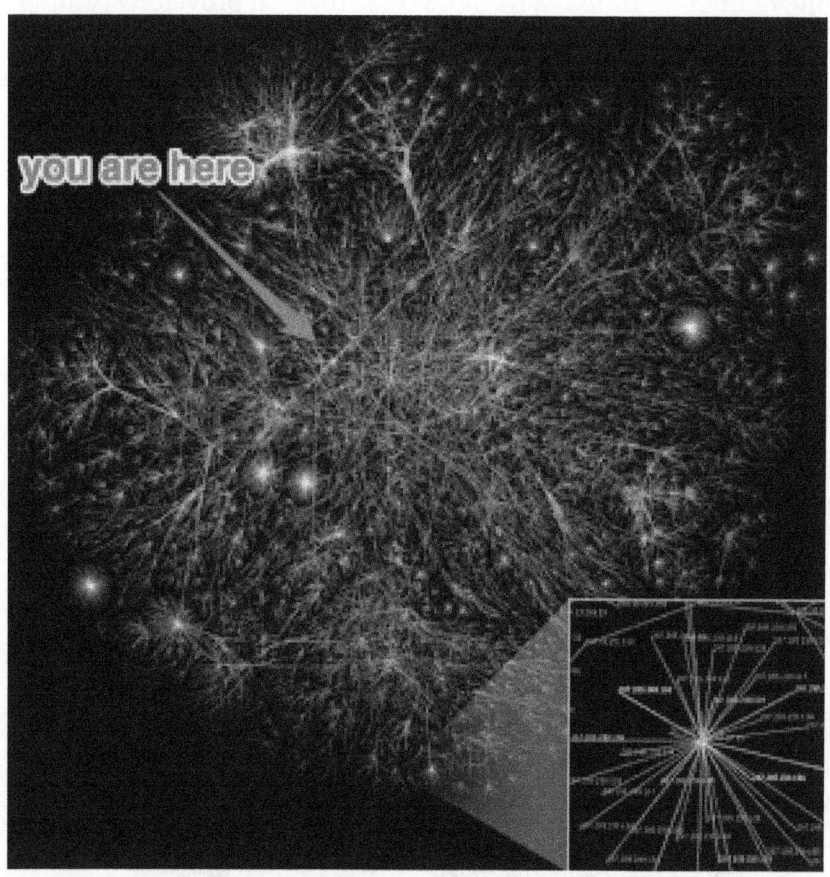

HTTP://EN.WIKIPEDIA.ORG/WIKI/NETWORK_MAPPING

The problem is that tools and strategies such as MOOCs, videos, virtual environments, and games are only as good as the contexts in which they are used. Even the most adept practitioners quickly discover that pressing emerging technology and culture into the shape of yesterday's curricular and instructional models amounts to little more than Skinner's Box 2.0.

So what is to be done? How can we use emerging tools and culture to deliver such an amazing individual and collaborative experience that it shatters expectations and helps students forget they're in school long enough to fall in love with learning again?

Education in the Information Age should enable learners to find, analyze, evaluate, curate, and act on the best available information. Pursuing an interdisciplinary path of inquiry in an interest-based community doesn't just facilitate the acquisition of factual knowledge (which has a limited half-life). The process brings learners closer to understanding their own habits of mind and gives them practice and an identity in the culture they'll be expected to join after they graduate. This requires new literacies and a curriculum that emphasizes mental fitness, physical fitness, spiritual fitness, civic fitness, and technological fitness.

Models of assessment that emphasize self-directed Paragogical and collaborative Peeragogical principles enrich the learning experience and accelerate and amplify deep understanding. Because these approaches are pull-based and generate tens of thousands of multi/transmedia data points per learner, they generate multi-dimensional portraits of learner development and provide feedback that goes far beyond strengths and weaknesses in content retention. The long-term benefit is exponential. Learners who can intentionally direct their own concentration are empowered far beyond knowledge acquisition or skill mastery. They become more effective thinkers and–because they are vested– more caring people. This learning experience is of their own making: it isn't business, it's personal. The inspiration to recreate the process for themselves and for others is the wellspring of the lifelong learner.

As Benjamin Disraeli put it, "In general the most successful man in life is the man who has the best information." It is a widely accepted truism in business that better data leads to better decisions. We now have the ability to generate, aggregate, analyze, and evaluate much richer data sets that can help us learn more about helping each other learn. Sharing different kinds of data in different ways will have the same game-changing effect in learning that it has in professional baseball, basketball, and investment banking.

Self-directed, collaborative assessment generates an unprecedented quantity and variety of data that illuminates aspects of learning, instruction, and overall systemic efficacy. Even a cursory examination of readily available freeware metrics, blog/social media content, and time stamps can provide valu-

Case Study: 5PH1NX

able insight into an individual's working process and differentiate learners in a network.

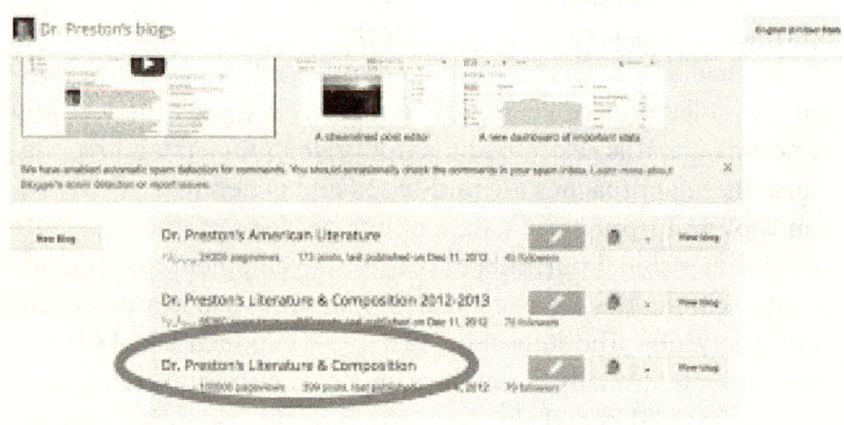

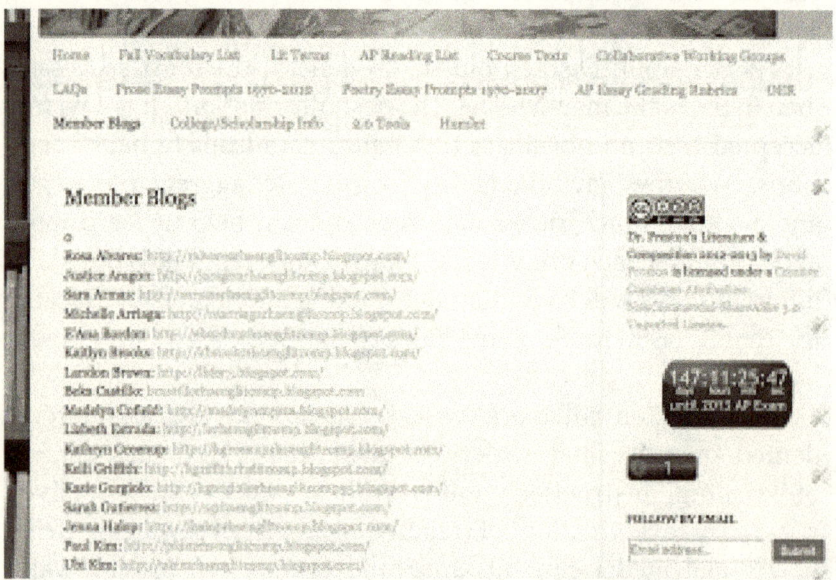

Case Study: 5PH1NX

Case Study: 5PH1NX

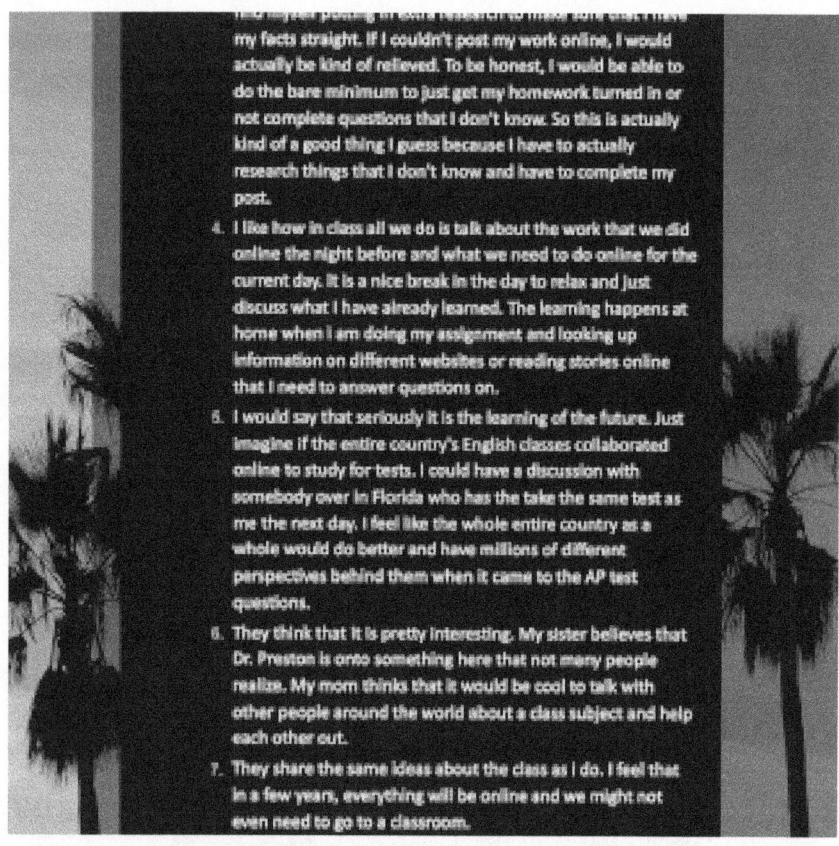

In the larger scheme of things, Peeragogical assessment provides direct access to and practice in the culture learners will be expected to join when they complete their course of study. Collaboration, delegation, facilitating conversations, and other highly valued skills are developed in plain view, where they can be critiqued and validated by peers, experts and the public.

SAMPLE EXERCISE: Flash Mob Mind Map

Learners responded to the assignment with real-time commentary and created a finished product in 24 hours. The map also attracted contributors outside the original learning community who lent perspectives on content, design and working process. Although there was no formal assessment process, it was easy for each viewer to see exactly who did what and how well.

But tall trees don't grow by themselves in the desert. Peeragogical innovation can be challenging in organizational cultures that prioritize control and standardization; as Senge et al have observed, the system doesn't evaluate quality when dealing with the unfamiliar, it just pushes back. In schools this is so typical that it doesn't merit comment in traditional media. The world notices when Syria goes dark, but in school restricted online access is business as usual.

Cultural constraints can make early adopters in technology-based Peeragogy seem like Promethean risk-takers. [1]

Learners are not fooled by the rhetoric of in loco parentis or vision statements that emphasize "safe, nurturing learning environments." With notable exceptions, today's school leaders do not know as much about technology as the young people for whom they assume responsibility. Still, learners understand survival: they are fighting in unfavorable terrain against an enemy of great power. Innovating is impossible and even loudly criticizing school or advocating for change is a risk. As a result many do just enough to satisfy requirements without getting involved enough to attract attention. Some have also internalized the critical voices of authority or the failure of the formal experience as evidence of their own inability: I'm just not any good at math.

How do we know when we're really good at something? Standardized testing feedback doesn't help learners improve. Most of us don't have a natural talent for offering or accepting criticism. And yet, as Wole Soyinka put it, "The greatest threat to freedom is the absence of criticism."? Peeragogical interaction requires refining relational and topical critique, as well as skills in other "meta" literacies, including but not limited to critical thinking, collaboration, conflict resolution, decision-making, mindfulness, patience and compassion.

Interpersonal learning skills are undervalued in today's schooling paradigm. Consequently there is an operational lack of incentive for teachers and learners to devote time and energy, particularly when it carries a perceived cost in achievement on tests that determine financial allocations and job security.[2]

Nevertheless, some educators are introducing peer-to-peer network language and even introducing peer-based assessment. But the contracts, syllabi and letters to students stink of the old ways. These one-to-many documents are presented by agents of the institution endowed with the power to reward or punish. To many students this does not represent a choice or a real opportunity to hack the learning experience. They suspect manipulation and they wait for the other shoe to drop. Learners also don't like to be told they're free while being forced to operate within tight constraints. Consider this reaction to a policy that is highly regarded in the field:

"Students may choose to reblog their work in a public place or on their own blogs, but do so at their own risk." What? Did I read that correctly? "Students may choose to reblog their work in a public place or on their own blogs, but do so at their own risk." Risk? What risk? The risk of possibly helping someone understand something that they didn't before or get a different opinion than they had before? Someone please help me make sense of this.

To effectively adopt Peeragogical assessment in the schooling context, the community must construct a new understanding of how the members in the network relate to one another independent of their roles in the surrounding social or hierarchical systems. This requires trust, which in school requires significant suspension of disbelief, which–and this is the hard part– requires actual substantive, structural change in the learning transaction. This is the defining characteristic of Open Source Learning: as the network grows, changes composition, and changes purpose, it also changes the direction and content of the learning experience. Every network member can introduce new ideas, ask questions, and contribute resources than refine and redirect the process.

Case Study: 5PH1NX

This isn't easy. A member in this network must forget what she knows about school in order to test the boundaries of learning that shape her relationship to content, peers, and expert sources of information and feedback. This is how the cogs in the machine become the liminal heroes who redesign it. Having rejected the old way, they must now create the rituals that will come to define the new. They are following in the path of Oedipus, who took on the inscrutable and intimidating Sphinx, solved the riddle that had killed others who tried, and ushered out the old belief systems to pave the way for the Gods of Olympus.

Imagine if Oedipus had the Internet.

NOTES

1. Whenever the author gives a talk or an interview someone asks if he's in trouble.

2. In recent years there has been increasing pressure to tie teacher compensation, performance evaluation, and job status to student performance on standardized tests.

3. Reminder: not so long ago this sentence would have been rightly interpreted as science fiction.

4. And its structure.

5. In [this year's version] students initially assigned symbolic literary value to the blue letters before the solution dawned & the comment thread ended with, "THA SCHEMEZ SCHEMEZ EVARYWARE."

Part IV

Peeragogy in Practice

CHAPTER 6

THINKING ABOUT PATTERNS

Authors: THE PEERAGOGY TEAM

Although a grounding in learning theory helps inform peer learning projects, Peeragogy, at its core, comes to life in applied practice. For a successful outcome, take a look at these best practices, patterns, and use cases (also called *case studies* or *examples*). Patterns and use cases that co-facilitators and participants identify as the project unfolds can serve the next peeragogical enterprise as well.

What is a pattern?

A pattern is anything that has a repeated effect. In the context of peeragogy, the practice is to repeat processes and interactions that advance the learning mission. Frequent occurrences that are not desirable are called anti-patterns!

> **Christopher Alexander**: "Each pattern describes a problems which occurs over and over again in our environment, and then describes the core of the solution to that problem, in a way that you can use this solution a million times over, without ever doing it the same way twice." [1]

Patterns provide a framework that can be applied to similar issues but may be metaphorically solved in different ways, sometimes in real world or face to face events and other times in digital space / applications.

> **Christopher Alexander**: "Can we do better? Does all this talk help to make better buildings? [...] What is the Chartres of programming? What task is at a high enough level to inspire people writing programs, to reach for the stars?" [2]

Note: the notion of the analog (such as a plaza) could become a digital metaphor for a group chat or Google+ Hangout – a group meeting space / agora. Indeed the working title for Google Communities was "piazza!"

Patterns of peeragogy

Here is our index of the patterns we've found so far (described in more detail after the jump):

- WRAPPER - Front end appearance to participants. Consolidate and summarize.

- DISCERNING A PATTERN - Found a pattern? Give it a title and example.

- POLLING FOR IDEAS - Invite brainstorming, collecting ideas, questions, and solutions.

- CREATING A GUIDE - Overviews expose the lay of the land. Collecting content and stories.

- NEWCOMER - Create a guide for "beginner's mind" and help avoid need to introduce new members each "meeting."

- ROADMAP - Plans for future work, direction towards a goal, dynamic

- ROLES - Specialize and mix it up. Play to participants strengths and skills.

- PROJECT FOCUS - Lightbulb moment: Most specific projects involve learning!

- CARRYING CAPACITY - Know your limits, find ways to get other people involved.

- HEARTBEAT - The "heartbeat" of the group keeps energy flowing.

- MODERATION - When leaders step back, dynamics can improve; moderator serves as champion and editor.

- USE OR MAKE? - Repurposing, tinkering, or creating from scratch?

- REITERATE - Periodically review and revise above actions as needed

Anti-patterns for Peeragogy

And some "anti-patterns" (things to avoid):

- ISOLATION - A tale of silos, holes, and not-invented-here.

- MAGICAL THINKING - "One meeting will (not) change everything!"

- MESSY WITH LURKERS - What happens when joining is low-cost and completion is low-benefit.

- MISUNDERSTANDING POWER - The workload is almost never evenly distributed.

- NAVEL GAZING - "I have this really great idea..."

- STASIS - What's the driver behind open source, commons-oriented collaborative projects? (Because, let's face it, it doesn't always work.)

- STUCK AT THE LEVEL OF WEAK TIES - can we deepen the connection?

What is a use case?

A use case describes someone (or something) who uses a given system or tool to achieve a goal. A use case can include a title, a summary of the problem, an actor, and a success scenario. Additional features can be added, such as alternate interactions or choices that lead to a variation on the result. The use case considers a given persona (a characteristic role) in a given situation and shows how they works on a project/problem and how their process of work is resolved into a solution or solutions. Some activities do not have a single solution – these are often referred to as "Wicked Problems." With detailed bookkeeping effort, recorded processes can be standardized into use cases that can then be employed directly or modified to fit the context of the activity at hand. In short, they are a lot like design patterns, which they may contain in hidden or explicit form. Use cases are presented in sidebars and vignettes that appear throughout the book (like the one below).

> John's day-job involves finding patterns in market data (see Kevin Slavin's TED talk). He reads philosophy and does some other programming work in his spare time. However, he doesn't take the Occupy Wall Street protest very seriously. But one of these evenings, one of the protestors catches his attention. She's dressed rather strikingly. They talk, and he comes away thinking about something she said: "*All our grievances are interconnected.*" What if all the solutions are interconnected too? Night time: John becomes increasingly obsessed with this idea. He's pulling down lots of web pages from the internet — again, looking for patterns. What would it take for OWS folks to solve the problems they worry so much about? He starts working on a tool that's geared towards learning and sharing skills, while working on real projects. At first, it's just hackers who are using the tool, but over time they adapt it for popular use.

Then things start to get interesting...

Pattern language

Combine patterns and use cases and you start to identify a PATTERN LANGUAGE that can be used immediately, and in future projects. The next section on PROBLEM SOLVING goes into more detail, but we'll preview the idea here with the following diagram:

The subsequent major sections of this book – *CONVENE*, *ORGANIZE*, *COOPERATE* and *ASSESS* – represent big clusters of patterns that are likely to come up time and again in various projects (do you see the analogy with the four major branches of the diagram above?). You are of course free to invent your own patterns. Each project will tend to have it's own design, and it's own unique way things play out in practice. Here, we present these small but powerful "starter patterns".

> **Christopher Alexander**: These ideas—patterns—are hardly more than glimpses of a much deeper level of structure, and is ultimately within this deeper level of structure, that the origin of life occurs.

EXAMPLES

The above use cases and patterns make the "story" abstract – but how about some concrete examples of peeragogy in action?

Consider:

- OPENHATCH.ORG, "an open source community aiming to help newcomers find their way into free software projects."

- The FREE TECHNOLOGY GUILD is a younger project with aspirations similar in some ways to those of OpenHatch, but in this case, oriented not just to pairing newcomers with mentors, but pairing clients with service providers. "The idea is that we as a group will do useful projects for our members or external parties, and on-the-job we mentor and learn and get better." (Since this is a new project, the PROJECT BUILDING PHASE is itself a nacent example of paragogy.)

- Many more examples on our EXAMPLES page!

References

1. Alexander, Christopher, Ishikawa, Sara, and Silverstein, Murray, *A Pattern Language: Towns, Buildings, and, Construction*, New York: Oxford University Press, 1977.

2. Gabriel, Richard P. PATTERNS OF SOFTWARE, New York: Oxford University Press, 1996. (Includes a forward by Christopher Alexander.)

Further readings on patterns

1. THE TIMELESS WAY OF BUILDING, by Christopher Alexander.

2. Article, "Manifesto 1991" by Christopher Alexander, Progressive Architecture, July 1991, pp. 108–112, provides a brief summary of Alexander's ideas in the form of a critique of mainstream architecture. Many of the same sorts of critical points would carry over to mainstream education. Some highlights are excerpted HERE.

3. WIKIPATTERNS

4. THE ORIGINS OF PATTERN THEORY, THE FUTURE OF THE THEORY, AND THE GENERATION OF A LIVING WORLD, Christopher Alexander's talk at the 1996 ACM Conference on Object-Oriented Programs, Systems, Languages and Applications (OOPSLA)

Other related work

1. CLUETRAIN MANIFESTO (the FIRST EDITION is available for free)

2. NEW RULES FOR THE NEW ECONOMY(YOU CAN ALSOREAD THE BOOK ONLINE)

CHAPTER 7

PATTERNS AND HEURISTICS

Ten potentially useful things to do when you're solving a problem are described by Artificial Intelligence pioneer Marvin Minsky in a series of MEMOS for the One Laptop Per Child project. We can sum them up visually with the following diagram:

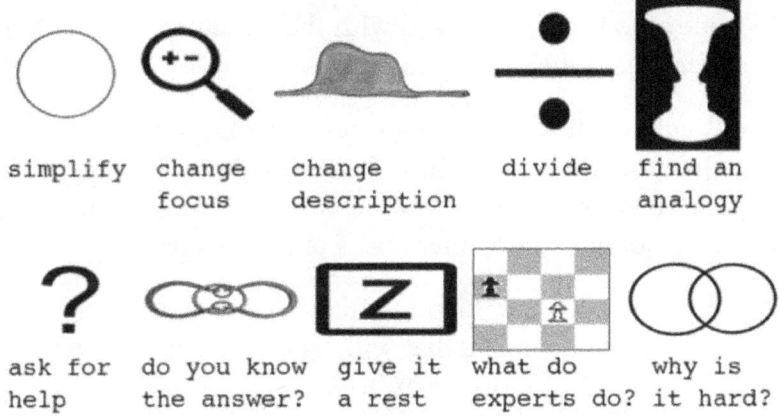

We can also see some interesting relationships to the peeragogy patterns we identified earlier. The connections are first described with a picture here, and then in more detail with text below. Some of the nodes in this diagram are clickable, and clicking will take you to the page describing the relevant pattern:

To elaborate in words:

- Simplify things for **Newcomers**. In practice, this means that we don't expect a newcomer to enter at full speed.

- Use a **Roadmap** to guide us from one phase to another, while the project's central **Heartbeat** helps us attend to the central focus.

- Announce changes through a **Wrapper** who describes the new status or direction of the project. For the Peeragogy project, that often meant summing up the high points that we saw over a given period of time.

- Assemble a **Pattern Language** for the project by first **Discerning Patterns**, and when we've seen how the patterns relate to each other (as in the diagram above), we can start to build a map like the one above, for subsequent use in problem-solving and design.

- We divide work up not only horizontally among different **Roles**, but also temporally by using the **Roadmap**. Someone who is moving ahead with the Roadmap is likely to be working at the leading edge.

- When we find an analogy, we are basically **Creating a Guide** of some sort. This can be used as a form of "exploration," as we look at how one form of engagement may or may not map onto other forms of engagement.

- When we ask for help, we may avail ourselves of some **Moderation** service that will decide how to deal with our request. One simple way to ask for help is **Polling for Ideas**. Obviously once we start to get help, we're working in a regime of "collaborative effort".

- If you know the answer, then you may be able to reuse it (which is the basic idea described in **Praxis vs Poesis**, though the title is a little bit obscure). Someone who knows the answer and who is good at self-explanation may also have a good idea about how to get from the current state to the goal state; alternatively, this may be broken down into steps in some sub-Roadmap, and moving from step to step would then illustrate "progressive problem solving".

- It is important to give it a rest so as not to over-exhaust oneself, busting one's own **Carrying Capacity**, or, alternatively, overwhelming the group.

- It seems that one of the things that experts do is **Discerning a Pattern**. This allows them to simplify their processing.

- Finally, again, if we know why it is hard, then we may be able to **Create a Guide** that will help get around, or at least better cope with, the difficulty.

Resources

- *The Society of Mind* is a book by Marvin Minsky that talks about how a mind can be made up of many different "agencies" that work together. A relatively recent review by Push Singh is AVAILABLE ONLINE, and contains a succinct overview of the key components of the more complex problem solving or "thinking" architecture described in Minsky's book.

- PEER SUPPORTED PROBLEM SOLVING AND MATHEMATICAL KNOWLEDGE is a forthcoming Ph. D. thesis by peeragogy co-author Joseph Corneli.

- Our STYLE GUIDE contains some guidelines to use when working on "problems of exposition"

CHAPTER 8

PATTERNS

Heartbeat

Without someone or something acting as the "heartbeat" for the group, energy may dissipate. In the "Collaborative Lesson Planning" course led by Charlie Danoff at P2PU (which I joined twice, and where we first talked through the ideas about paragogy), Charlie wrote individual emails to people who were signed up for the course and who had disappeared, or lurked but didn't participate. This kept some of us (including me!) making positive contributions. - *Joe Corneli*

Carrying Capacity

> *"If overstimulation at the sensory level increases the distortion with which we perceive reality, cognitive overstimulation interferes with our ability to 'think.'"* – Future Shock, by Alvin Toffler

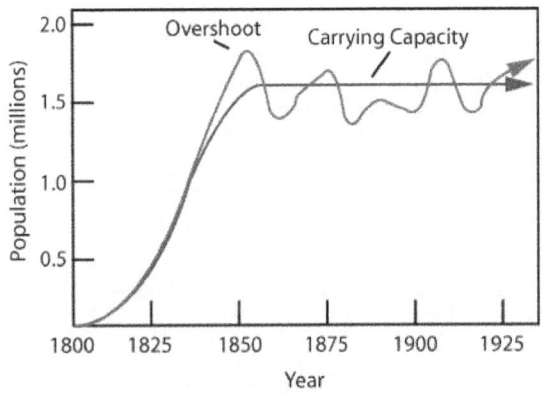

Image from MISS BAKER'S BIOLOGY CLASS WIKI (CC-By-NC-SA).

At times, a facilitator or participant in the peer-learning enterprise may feel he or she is over-contributing – or, perhaps more likely, that others are under-contributing – or that someone else is railroading an idea or dominating the discussion. If this happens, take a step back and observe the dynamics of involvement. Ask questions and let others answer. Especially if you start to feel the symptoms of burnout, it's important that you find the level of engagement that allows you to participate at a level that is feasible for maintaining progress toward the project's goal. Lead by example – but make sure it's someplace you, and others, actually want to go! This could be a good time to revisit the group's roadmap and see if you can figure out and clarify to others what concrete goal you're working towards. Remember that you can also change the "landscape" by making it easier for other people to get involved – for example, by explaining what you're trying to do in a clear manner. Watch for opportunities to step back, watch, listen. Try to be mindful of phases when active or quiet involvement would be more helpful to the individual and the group. It's also helpful to let anyone who has taken on a facilitation role know if you're stepping back temporarily. Then, when the time is right, step back in and get to work!

Creating a Guide

Meaning-carrying tools, like handbooks or maps, can help people use an idea. In particular, when the idea or system is only "newly discovered", the associated meanings may not be well understood (indeed they may not have been created). In such a case, the process of creating the guide can go hand-in-hand with figuring out how the system works. Thus, techniques of KNOWLEDGE CARTOGRAPHY and MEANING MAKING are useful for would-be guide creators. Even so, it is worth noting that "the map is not the territory," and map-making is only one facet of shared human activity. Collaboratively refining a pattern is itself an example of "Creating a Guide" - that is, a pattern description can be thought of as a "micro-map" of a specific activity.

Discerning a Pattern

Discerning patterns helps us build our vocabulary or repertoire for peer-learning projects.

> [W]e saw that language use is typically what we have to go on, from an analytical perspective. Generally, if we are not starting with language, we arrive at it soon enough. Language becomes something to pay attention to, in much the same way in which Buddhist practitioners have for centuries spent time watching their breath.
> — From "PARAGOGICAL PRAXIS" by Joe Corneli

The challenge of discerning a peeragogical pattern revolves around a meta-awareness of language. For example, in building a peer learning profile, a participant might identify an interest such as organic gardening. We notice this is a pattern when it repeats; when organic gardening is frequently listed among interests listed by participants in their introductions. The classic example of a pattern is "a place to wait" —a type of space found in many architectural and urban design projects. Once a pattern is detected, give it a title and write down how the pattern works in a peer learning context. What does this pattern say about the self-selection process of the group? Without jumping to conclusions, consider that an interest in organic gardening, for example, *might* indicate the participants are oriented to cooperation, personal health, or environmental activism (emphasis on *might!*).

Moderation

> "Why is a fishbowl more productive than debate? The small group conversations in the fishbowl tend to depersonalize the issue and reduce the stress level, making people's statements more cogent. Since people are talking with their fellow partisans, they get less caught up in wasteful adversarial games." - the Co-INTELLIGENCE INSTITUTE

Participation in online forums tends to follow a "power law," with unequal engagement. One remedy for this is simply for the most active participants to step back, and moderate how much they speak (see Carrying Capacity). OWS uses a similar technique in their "progressive stack."

Newcomer

> Unless there is a new person to talk to, a lot of the "education stuff" we do could grow stale. Many of the patterns and use cases for peeragogy assume that there will be an audience or a new generation of learners - hence the drive to create a *guide*. Note that the *newcomer* and the *wrapper* may work together to make the project accessible. Even in the absence of actual newcomers, we're often asked to try and look at things with a "beginner's mind."

Newcomers can provide constructive (sometimes critical) feedback on the way a project is organized.

> **Régis Barondeau:** I joined this handbook project late, making me a "newcomer". When I started to catch up, I rapidly faced doubts:
>
> - Where do I start?
> - How can I help?
> - How will I make it, having to read more than 700 posts?
> - What tools are we using ? How do I use them?
> - Etc.
>
> Even if this project is amazingly interesting, catching the train while it already reached high speed can be an extreme sport. By taking care of newcomers, we might avoid loosing valuable contribuors because

they don't know how and where to start, and keep our own project on the track, if we are able to explain the project to newcomers. Some ideas about things we could do better:

- Allow participants to see the whole, for example by having a project landing page, by using dynamic mindmapping of wiki pages, etc.
- Have mentors that will guide newcomers for some time. They could for example kickstart them by showing where there expertise may fit into the project.
- Have landing pages overviews for every sub-project. This overview could show : who is involved, what are the main objectives, what tools are used (assuming sub-project teams may use some specific tools), etc.
- Have tools introduction and if possible support. In this project we all seem to be used to online tools but this is often not the case.
- Create a newcomer wiki page listing the basics.

Charlotte Pierce: Joe Corneli's EXAMPLE evoked my own experience energing the Peeragogy community. Joe was working a lot on the book, and I thought "this is interesting hard work, and he shouldn't have to do this alone." As a Peeragogy newcomer, I was kindly welcomed and mentored by Joe, Howard, Fabrizio, and others. I asked naive questions and was met with patient answers, guiding questions, and resource links. Concurrently, I bootstrapped myself into a position to contribute to the workflow by editing the live manuscript for consistency, style, and continuity. The concrete act of editing and fact-checking this relatively (to me) unfamiliar topic in physical isolation rapidly raised my understanding of the field. I also returned to the SOCIAL MEDIA CLASSROOM forums to follow up on early offers of editing help from recently uninvolved particpants, resulting in the rekindled interest of several new editors (if not an overwhelming army).

Additional Reading

1. WHY DO NEWCOMERS ABANDON OPEN SOURCE SOFTWARE PROJECTS? (sildes by Igor Steinmacher and coauthors)

Pattern Language

I use the idea of a *pattern language* as a shorthand for what Christopher Alexander talks about in his KEYNOTE ADDRESS for the IEEE in 1996.

In short, once we have come up with enough patterns (including the pattern of a *pattern language* that I discussing here, and its generalizations per Christopher Alexander), then we will be better able to do both the socio-technical design work associated with planning pæragogical experiences, and, quite likely, enjoy the "actual work" more too.

In this quote from the linked article, C. A. talks about computer programming, but I think the same could go for any other sort of design-and-implementation work:

> *It is a view of programming as the natural genetic infrastructure of a living world which you/we are capable of creating, managing, making available, and which could then have the result that a living structure in our towns, houses, work places, cities, becomes an attainable thing. That would be remarkable. It would turn the world around, and make living structure the norm once again, throughout society, and make the world worth living in again. This is an extraordinary vision of the future, in which computers play a fundamental role in making the world - and above all the built structure of*

> the world - alive, humane, ecologically profound, and with a deep living structure.

Polling for Ideas

... and then Howard said *"At the beginning, until we all know the ropes well enough to understand when to create a new discussion forum topic and when to add to an existing one, let's talk in this topic thread about what else we want to discuss and I will start new topic threads when necessary."* Polling for Ideas can happen at many junctures in a peer learning experience, e.g. we could poll for ideas about "who would we like to join our group?", and "what would be good resources for us to use?"

Praxis vs Poeisis

> "Praxis, a noble activity, is always one of use, as distinct from poesis which designates fabrication. Only the former, which plays and acts, but does not produce, is noble." [1] (p. 101)

There is a tension between "making stuff" (*poesis*) and "using stuff" (*praxis*). Peer *production*, as the name indicates, is about "making stuff." And making stuff can be fun. But we should also ask ourselves, how much new stuff do we really need? There's not a hard and fast answer to that. We should also consider how much "learning" is really "remix" – that is, re-use and recycling of other people's ideas and techniques.

Understanding and negotiating the tension between reuse and creativity is the key to *the art of remix* or "paragogical praxis"!

Reference

1. Baudrillard, J. (1975). *The mirror of production.* Telos Press

19th century collage cards, care of NICK HAUS

Focusing on a specific project

In the Jan. 2013 plenary session, as INDEPENDENT PUBLISHERS OF NEW ENGLAND (IPNE) President Tordis Isselhardt quietly listed to the presentation of how we created the Peeragogy Handbook. During the Q&A, Isselhardt spoke up and wondered if peer-learning effort in IPNE might be more likely to succeed if the organization's members "focused around a specific project." As this lightbulb illuminated the room, those of us attending the plenary session suggested that IPNE could focus the project by creating an "Independent Publishing Handbook." (applause). In the course of creating the IPNE Handbook, peer learners would assemble resource repositories, exchange expertise, and collaboratively edit documents. To provide motivation and incentive to participate in PeerPubU, members of the association will earn authorship credit for contributing articles, editor credit for working on the manuscript, and can spin off their own chapters as stand-alone, profit-making publications. See plenary session video.

Roadmap

It is very useful to have an up-to-date public roadmap for the project, someplace where it can be discussed and maintained. This helps NEWCOMERS see where they can jump in. It also gives a sense of the accomplishments to date, and any major challenges that lie ahead. Remember, the Roadmap exists as an artifact with which to share current, but never complete, understanding of the space. Never stop learning!

Examples

In the Peeragogy project, once the book's outline became fairly mature, we could use it as a roadmap, by marking the sections that are "finished" (at least in draft), marking the sections where editing is currently taking place, and marking the stubs (possible starting points for future contributors). After this outline matured into a real TABLE OF CONTENTS, we started to look in other directions for ways to build on our successes to date, and started working on a ROADMAP FOR FURTHER DEVELOPMENT OF THE WEBSITE AND PEERAGOGY PROJECT AS A WHOLE.

And also

Note that a shared roadmap is very similar to a PERSONAL LEARNING PLAN, or "paragogical profile". We've made some EXAMPLES of these as we got started working on the Free Technology Guild.

There is a certain roadmappiness to "presentation of self", and you can learn to use this well. For instance, when introducing yourself and your work to other people, you can focus on highlights like these:

- "What is the message behind what you're doing?"

- "How do you provide a model others can follow or improve upon?"

- "How can others get directly involved with your project?"

Roles

This may seem like an obvious one, but educational interactions tend to have a number of different roles associated with them. Consider that everything could bifurcate from the "autodidact": 1. Autodidact 2. Tutor-Tutee 3. Tutor-Tutee-Parent 5. Tutor-Tutee #1-Tutee #2-Parent-Principal etc., until we have bursars, librarians, technicians, janitors, editors of peer reviewed research journals, government policy makers, spin-off industrial ventures and partnerships, etc., all involved in Education. Even the autodidact may assume different roles at different points in time - sometimes making a library run, sometimes constructing a model, sometimes checking a proof. The decomposition of "learning" into different phases or polarities could be an endless theoretical task. For the moment, we just note that roles are often present "by default" at the start of a learning process, and that they may change as the process develops.

Wrapper

Early on, active peeragogue Charlie Danoff SUGGESTED that someone take on the "wrapper role" – do a weekly pre/post wrap, so that new users would know the status the project is at any given point in time. The project wiki MAIN PAGE also serves as a "wrapper", and in Peeragogy, we check it from time to time to make sure that it accurately represents the basic facts about the project. Note that the "wrapper role" is similar to the integrative function that is needed for commons-based peer production to work (according to the theory proposed by Yochai Benkler, it is vital to have both 1) the ability to contribute small pieces; 2) some "integrative function" that stitches those pieces together. In Peeragogy, the Weekly Roundup" by Christopher Tillman Neal served to engage and re-engage members. Peeragogues began to eager watched for the weekly reports to see if our teams or our names had been mentioned. When there was a holiday or break, Chris would announce the hiatus, to keep the flow going.

CHAPTER 9

ANTIPATTERNS

Isolation

> **Félix Guattari:** *Imagine a fenced field in which there are horses wearing adjustable blinkers, and let's say that the "coefficient of transversality" will be precisely the adjustment of the blinkers. If the horses are completely blind, a certain kind of traumatic encounter will be produced. As soon as the blinkers are opened, one can imagine that the horses will move about in a more harmonious way.* (QUOTED BY ANDREW MURPHY, himself quoting Gary Genosko)

From a design point of view: we should be conscious of interfaces that are "too loud", and think about how that is compensated for by isolation of various forms. With a too-narrow focus, people end up bumping into each other uncomfortably. However, with an over-wide focus, things are chaotic in other ways (see

Co-Learning: Messy with Lurkers), motivating a narrowing of focus. An effort that isolates itself will not have the occasion to draw on other resources.

This sometimes goes by the name *Not Invented Here*. But focus is really only a problem when it becomes overfocus, resulting in uncomfortable bumps. When that happens, it seems like a good reason to try to clarify how to engage in a more fruitful manner. Learning how to manage the uncertainty that comes with experimentation is part of what makes the postmodern organization tick! (See also: Participatory Design vs Navel Gazing.)

Magical thinking

Introduction

While the ideal platform would (magically) come with solutions pre-built, a more realistic approach recognizes that problem solving always takes time and energy. The problem solving approach and associated "learning orientation" will also depend on the task and resources at hand. [...] Arguably, if we "knew", 100%, how to do peeragogy, then we would not stand to learn very much by writing this handbook. Difficulties and tensions would be resolved "in advance" (see earlier comments about "magical" technologies for peer production).

Magical Thinking is the thief of process

Magical thinking of the kind described above robs a context of its "process" (Nishida might say, its "motion"). It seems possible that the more structure we have "in advance", and the more we can fall back on "traditional" modes of doing things, the less we stand to learn. I quote at length:

> *"Optimization of decision-making processes confers an important advantage in response to a constantly changing environment. The ability to select the appropriate actions on the basis of their consequences and on*

our needs at the time of the decision allows us to respond in an efficient way to changing situations. However, the continuous control and attention that this process demands can result in an unnecessary expenditure of resources and can be inefficient in many situations. For instance, when behavior is repeated regularly for extensive periods without major changes in outcome value or contingency, or under uncertain situations where we cannot manipulate the probability of obtaining an outcome, general rules and habits can be advantageous. Thus, the more rapid shift to habits after chronic stress could be a coping mechanism to improve performance of well-trained behaviors, while increasing the bioavailability to acquire and process new information, which seems essential for adaptation to complex environments. However, when objectives need to be re-updated in order to make the most appropriate choice, the inability of stressed subjects to shift from habitual strategies to goal-directed behavior might be highly detrimental. Such impairment might be of relevance to understand the high comorbidity between stress-related disorders and addictive behavior or compulsivity, but certainly has a broader impact spanning activities from everyday life decisions to economics." – Science Magazine

This also has interesting implications when it comes to "detecting learning" (see "RESEARCHING PEERAGOGY"). How do emotions, stress, learning, habit, and adaptation relate?

Messy with Lurkers

Gigi Johnson: *(1) Co-learning is Messy. It needs time, patience, confusion, re-forming, re-norming, re-storming, etc. Things go awry and part of norms needs to be how to realign. (2) Co-learning is a VERY dif-*

ferent experience from traditional teacher-led learning in terms of time and completion. It is frustrating, so many people will lurk or just step in and out, the latter of which is very different from what is acceptable in traditonal learning. Online learning programs are painted with the brush now of an "unacceptable" 50% average non-completion rate. Stanford's MOOC AI class, which started out with +100,000 people, had 12% finish. If only 12% or 50% of my traditional class finished, I'd have a hard time getting next quarter's classes approved!

The second point is similar to the earlier Anti-pattern "MISUNDERSTANDING POWER (LAWS)". People have to join in order to try, and when joining is low-cost, and completion low-benefit, it is not surprising that many people will "dissipate" as the course progresses. The "messiness" of co-learning is interesting because it points to a sort of "internal dissipation", as contributors bring their multiple different backgrounds, interests, and communication styles to bear. In TOMLINSON ET AL., we observed:

More authors means more content, but also more words thrown away. Many of the words written by authors were deleted during the ongoing editing process. The sheer mass of deleted words might raise the question of whether authoring a paper in such a massively distributed fashion is efficient.

If we were to describe this situation in traditional subject/object terms, we would say that peer production has a "low signal to noise ratio". However, it may be more appropriate (and constructive) to think of meanings as co-constructed as the process runs, and of messiness (or meaninglessness) as symptomatic, not of peer production *itself*, but of deficiencies or infelicities in shared meaning-making and "integrating" features.

Misunderstanding Power

> Zipf's law states that given some corpus of natural language utterances, the frequency of any word is inversely proportional to its rank in the frequency table. Thus the most frequent word will occur approximately twice as often as the second most frequent word, three times as often as the third most frequent word, etc.

Zipf's law (or other formulations of the same thing) govern the SIZE OF CITIES, and related formulations describe ENERGY USE: roughly speaking, an elephant has a lower metabolism than a mouse and is more "energy efficient". At that same link, we see the suggestion that creativity in large-scale environments *speeds up!* *The anti-pattern*: how many times have we been at a conference or workshop and heard someone say (or said ourselves) "wouldn't it be great if this energy could be sustained all year 'round?" Or in a classroom or peer production setting, wondered why it is that everyone does not participate equally. "Wouldn't it be great if we could increase participation?" If you believe the result above, large-scale participation would indeed tend to increase creativity! - But nevertheless, participation does tend to fall off according to *some* power law (see Introduction to Power Laws in THE UNCERTAINTY PRINCIPLE, VOLUME II, ISSUE 3), and it would be a grand illusion to assume that everyone is coming from a similar place with regard to the various literacies and motivations that are conducive to participation. Furthermore, a "provisionist" attitude ("If we change our system we will equalize participation and access") simply will not work in general, *since power laws are inherently an epiphenomenon of networks*. Note that participation in a given activity often (but not always) falls off over *time* as well. This effect seems related but is also not well understood (many people would like to write a hit song / best selling novel / start a religion / etc., but few actually do). See the antipattern "MAGICAL THINKING" for more on that. *About the title*: Note that those agents who do post the most in a given collaboration (respectively, the words or ideas that are most common in a given language) will tend to influence the space the most. In this way, we can see some parallels between the SAPIR-WHORF HYPOTHESIS and Bourdieu's notion of "SYMBOLIC VIOLENCE". Much as Paul Graham wrote about programming languages – programmers are typically "satisfied with whatever language they happen to use, because it dictates the way they think about programs" – so too are people often "satisfied" with their social environments, because these tend to dictate the way they think and act in life.

Navel Gazing

The difficulty I am referring to breaks down like this:

1. Certainly we cannot get things done just by talking about them.

2. And yet, feedback *can* be useful, i.e., if there are mechanisms for responding to it in a useful fashion.

3. The associated *anti-pattern* is a special case of the prototypical Bateson DOUBLE BIND, "the father who says to his son, go ahead and criticize me - with the strong hint that all effective criticism will be very unwelcome."

Indeed – criticism is not always useful. Sometimes it is just "noise". *The art of paragogical praxis is to make something useful out of what would otherwise just be noise.*

Stasis

Actually, of course, living beings are never *really* in stasis. It just sometimes feels that way. Different anti-patterns like ISOLATION or NAVEL-GAZING have described different aspects of the *experience* of feeling like one is in stasis. Typically, what is happening in such a case is that one or more dimensions of life are moving very slowly. For instance, it seems we are not able to get programming support to improve this version of the Social Media

Classroom, for love or money, since all developer energy is going into the next version. This isn't true stasis, but it can feel frustrating when a specific small feature is desired, but unavailable. The solution? Don't get hung up on small things, and find the dimensions where movement *is* possible. In a sense this is analogous to eating a balanced diet. You probably shouldn't only eat grilled cheese sandwiches, even if you like them a lot. You should go for something different once in a while. This is also related to the pattern that talks about "Carrying Capacity". There is always some dimension on which you can make progress – it just might not be the same dimension you've recently over-harvested!

Stuck at the level of weak ties

Remember this from our article on organizing a learning context?

> *There is a certain irony here: we are studying "peeragogy", and yet many respondents did not feel they were really getting to know one another "as peers". Several remarked that they learned less from other individual participants, and more from "the collective". Those who did have a "team", or who knew one another from previous experiences, felt more peer-like in those relationships.*

Are weak ties "strong"?

"Weak ties" are often deemed a strength: see for example this article in Psychology Today, which says:

> "[S]trong and weak ties tend to serve different functions in our lives. When we need a big favor or social or instrumental support, we ask our friends. We call them when we need to move a washing machine. But if we need information that we don't have, the people to ask are our weak ties. They have more diverse knowledge

> *and more diverse ties than our close friends do. We ask them when we want to know who to hire to install our washing machine."*

The quote suggests that there is a certain trade-off between use of weak ties and use of strong ties. The anti-pattern in question then is less to do with whether we are forming weak ties or strong ties, and more to do with whether we are being *honest with ourselves and with each other about the nature of the ties we are forming* – and their potential uses. We can be "peers" in either a weak or a strong sense. The question to ask is whether our needs match our expectations!

In the peeragogy context, this has to do with how we interact. One of the participants in this project wrote:

> *"I am learning about peeragogy, but I think I'm failing [to be] a good peeragog[ue]. I remember that Howard [once] told us that the most important thing is that you should be responsible not only for your own learning but for your peers' learning. [...] So the question is, are we learning from others by ourselves or are we [...] helping others to learn?"*

If we are "only" co-consumers of information (which happens to "produced" live, by some of the participants), then this seems like a classic example of a weak tie. We are part of the same "audience" – or anyway, in the same "theater" (even if separated from each other by continuous "4th walls"). On the other hand, actively engaging with other people (whether with "my" learning, with "their" learning, or with the co-production of knowledge) seems to be the foundation for strong ties. In this case our aims (or needs) are more instrumental, and less informational.

People who do not put in the time and effort will remain stuck at the level of "weak ties", and will not be able to draw on the benefits that "strong ties" offer.

Part V

Convening A Group

CHAPTER 10

BUILDING YOUR CO-LEARNING GROUP

Authors: GIGI JOHNSON and JOE CORNELI

So you want to try peer learning? Maybe you've already found a few people who will support you in this effort. Congratulations! It's time now to focus your thinking. How will you convene others to form a suitable group? How will you design a learner experience which will make your project thrive? In this chapter, we suggest a variety of questions that will help you to make your project more concrete for potential new members. There are no good or bad answers - it depends on the nature of your project and the context. Trying to answer the questions is not something you do just once. At various stages of the project, even after it's over, some or all of those questions will aquire new meanings - and probably new answers.

FABRIZIO TERZI: *"There is a force of attraction that allows aggregation into groups based on the degree of personal interest; the ability to enhance and improve the share of each participant; the expectation of success and potential benefit."*

Group identity

Note that there are many groups that may not need to be "convened", since they already exist. There is a good story from A. T. ARIYARATNE in his COLLECTED WORKS in which he does "convene" a natural group (namely, a village) - but in any case, keep in mind at the outset that the degree of group-consciousness that is necessary for peer learning to take place is not fixed. In this section, we suppose you are just at the point of kicking off a project. What steps should you take? We suggest you take a moment to ponder the following questions first - and revisit them afterward, as a way to identify best practices for the next effort.

There will be a quiz

Those taking the initiative should ask themselves the traditional Who, What, Where, When, Why, and How. (SIMON SINEK suggests to begin with Why, and we touched on Who, above!). In doing so, preliminary assumptions for design and structure are established. However, in peer learning it is particularly important to maintain a healthy degree of openness, so that future group members can also form their answers on those questions. In particular, this suggests that the design and structure of the project (and the group) may change over time. Here, we riff on the traditional 5W's+H with six clusters of questions to help you focus your thinking about the project and amplify its positive outcomes.

"I keep six honest serving-men (They taught me all I knew)"

Expectations for participants

Once he gets to the Whispering Gallery, Roland realizes that the girl was right. This *is* the center of the universe. There are murmurs to be heard there – it seems they come from everywhere. He hears about guilds and the craftsmen who built the cathedral. He learns about how proud they were and how they formed communities of practice, educating the uninitiated, teaching each other to create. He returns to ground level. The girl is gone, but yet he feels happy. He realizes he can do more then repackage the social media streams, that there is more than twitter as a new broadcast medium. He starts a new journey: finding a guild, a community of practice, but restyled in a 21st century fashion. It will be more open, more connected to others then the old guilds. He will still use twitter, a social dashboard, and curating tools, but also he uses wikis, and synchronous communication. And most importantly, he starts building, together with others – in particular, together with the people formerly known as his readers. They will co-create the analysis, the search for solutions and sense-making, rather than helplessly listening to "experts", passively consuming the knowledge and information. Instead, they'll start building their own destiny as a community, and the newsroom will be part of the platform.

1. Who: Roles and flux

- What are some of the roles that people are likely to fall into (e.g. Newcomer, Wrapper, Lurker, Aggregator, etc.)?

- How likely is it that participants will stick with the project? If you expect many participants to leave, how will this effect the group and the outcome?

- Do you envision new people joining the group as time goes by? If so, what features are you designing that will support their integration into an existing flow?

- Will the project work if people dip in and out? If so, what features support that? If not, how will people stay focused?

2. What: Nature of the project

- What skills are required? What skills are you trying to build?

- What kinds of change will participants undergo? Will they be heading into new ground? Changing their minds about something? Learning about learning?

- What social objective, or "product" if any, is the project aiming to achieve?

- What's the 'hook?' Unless you are working with an existing group, or re-using an existing modality, consistent participation may not be a given.

3. When: Time management

- What do you expect the group to do, from the moment it convenes, to the end of its life-span, to create the specific outcome that will exist at the conclusion of its last meeting? (C. Gersick.) Note that what people ACTUALLY do may be different from what you envision at the outset, so you may want to revisit this question (and your answer) again as the project progresses.

- Keeping in mind that at least one period of is inertia is very likely (C. Gersick), what event(s) do you anticipate happening in the group that will bring things back together, set a new direction, or generally get things on track? More generally, what kinds of contingencies does your group face? How does it interface to the "outside world"?

- What pre-existing narratives or workflows could you copy in your group?

- How much of a time commitment do you expect from participants? Is this kind of commitment realistic for members of your group?

- What, if anything, can you do to make participation "easy" in the sense that it happens in the natural flow of life for group members?

- Does everyone need to participate equally? How might non-equal participation play out for participants down the line?

4. Where: Journey vs Destination

- What structures will support participants in their journey to the end result(s) you (or they) have envisioned? What content can you use to flesh out this structure?

- Where can the structure "flex" to accommodate unknown developments or needs as participants learn, discover, and progress?

5. Why: Tool/platform choice

- What tools are particularly suited to this group? Consider such features as learning styles and experiences, geographical diversity, the need for centralization (or decentralization), cultural expectations related to group work, sharing, and emerging leadership.

- Is there an inherent draw to this project for a given population, or are you as facilitator going to have to work at keeping people involved? How might your answer influence your choice of tools? Is the reward for completion the learning itself, or something more tangible?

- In choosing tools, how do you prioritize such values and objectives as easy entry, diverse uses, and high ceilings for sophisticated expansion?

6. How: Linearity vs Messiness

- How will your group manage feedback in a constructive way?

- Why might participants feel motivated to give feedback?

- How firm and extensive are the social contracts for this group? Do they apply to everyone equally, or do they vary with participation level?

- What do people need to know at the start? What can you work out as you go along? Who decides?

- How welcome are "meta-discussions"? What kinds of discussions are not likely to be welcome? Do you have facilities in place for "breakout groups" or other peer-to-peer interactions? (Alternatively, if the project is mostly distributed, do you have any facilities in place for coming together as a group?)

Cycles of group development

The above questions remain important thoughout the life of the project. People may come and go, particpants may propose fundamentally new approaches, people may evolve from lurkers to major content creators or vice-versa. The questions we suggest can be most effective if your group discusses them over time, as part of its workflow, using synchronous online meetings (e.g., BIG BLUE BUTTON, ADOBE CONNECT, BLACKBOARD COLLABORATE), forums, Google docs, wikis, and/or email lists. Regular meetings are one way to establish a "heartbeat" for the group.

In thinking about other ways of structuring things, note that the "body" of the *Peeragogy Handbook* follows a TUCKMAN-LIKE OUTLINE (*Convening a Group* is our "forming", *Organizing a Learning Context* is our "storming and norming", *Co-working/Facilitation* is our "performing", and *Assessment* is our "adjourning"). But we agree with Gersick (and Engeström) that groups do not always follow a linear or cyclical pattern with their activities!

Nevertheless, there may be some specific stages or phases that you want *your* group to go through. Do you need some "milestones," for example? How will you know when you've achieved "success?"

Dealing with chaos or conflict

In closing, it is worth reminding you that it is natural for groups to experience conflict, especially as they grow or cross other threshold points or milestones - or perhaps more likely, when they don't cross important milestones in a timely fashion (ah, so you remember those milestones from the previous section!). Nevertheless, there are some strategies can be used to make this conflict productive, rather than merely destructive (see Ozturk and Simsek).

Recommended Reading

1. Engeström, Y. (1999). Innovative learning in work teams: Analyzing cycles of knowledge creation in practice. In Y. Engeström, R. Miettinen & R.-L-. Punamäki (Eds.), *Perspectives on activity theory*, (pp. 377-404). Cambridge, UK: Cambridge University Press

2. Gersick, C. (1988). Time and transition in work teams: Toward a new model of group development. *Academy of Management Journal* 31 (Oct.): 9-41.

3. Mimi Ito's observations about MANGA FAN GROUPS CO-LEARNING JAPANESE

4. Rheingold U, MINDAMP GROUPS

5. Shneiderman, B. (2007). CREATIVITY SUPPORT TOOLS: ACCELERATING DISCOVERY AND INNOVATION. *Commun. ACM* 50, 12 (December 2007), 20-32. doi:10.1145/1323688.1323689,

6. Tomlinson, B., Ross, J., André, P., Baumer, E.P.S., Patterson, D.J., Corneli, J., Mahaux, M., Nobarany, S., Lazzari, M., Penzenstadler, B., Torrance, A.W., Callele, D.J., Olson, G.M., Silberman, M.S., Ständer, M., Palamedi, F.R., Salah, A., Morrill, E., Franch, X., Mueller, F., Kaye, J., Black, R.W., Cohn, M.L., Shih, P.C., Brewer, J., Goyal, N., Näkki, P., Huang, J., Baghaei, N., and Saper, C., MASSIVELY DISTRIBUTED AUTHORSHIP OF ACADEMIC PAPERS, *Proceedings of Alt.Chi, Austin Texas, May 5–10 2012* (10 page extended abstract), ACM, 2012,

7. David de Ugarte, Phyles. (SUMMARY) (BOOK)

8. Scheidel, T. M., & Crowell, L. (1964). Idea development in small discussion groups. *Quarterly Journal of Speech*, 50, 140-145.

9. Scheidel, T. M., & Crowell, L. (1979), *Discussing and Deciding - A Desk Book for Group Leaders and Members*, Macmillan Publishing

10. Ozturk and Simsek, "Of Conflict in Virtual Learning Communiities in the Context of a Democratic Pedagogy: A paradox or sophism?," in *Proceedings of the Networked Learning Conference, 2012, Maastricht*. VIDEO orTEXT.

11. Paragogy Handbook, HOW TO ORGANIZE A MOOC

12. Cathy Davidson et al., HOW A CLASS BECOMES A COMMUNITY

CHAPTER 11

PLAY AND LEARNING

Once more we're back to the question, "What makes learning fun?" There are deep links between play and learning. Consider, for instance, the way we learn the rules of a game through playing it. The first times we play a card game, or a physical sport, or a computer simulation we test out rule boundaries as well as our understanding. Actors and role-players learn their roles through the dynamic process of performance. The resulting learning isn't absorbed all at once, but accretes over time through an emergent process, one unfolding further through iterations. In other words, the more we play a game, the more we learn it.

In addition to the rules of play, we learn about the subject which play represents, be it a strategy game (chess, for example) or simulation of economic conflict. Good games echo good teaching practice, too, in that they structure a single player's experience to fit their regime of competence (cf. Vygotsky's zone of proximal learning, a la Gee [1]). That is to say a game challenges players at a level suited to their skill and knowledge: comfortable enough that play is possible, but so challenging as to avoid boredom, eliciting player growth. Role-playing in theater lets performers explore and test out concepts; see Boal [2]. Further, adopting a playful attitude helps individuals meet new challenges with curiosity, along with a readiness to mobilize ideas and practical knowledge. Indeed, the energy activated by play can take a person beyond an event's formal limitations, as players can assume that play can go on and on [3].

Douglas Thomas and John Seely Brown: "All systems of play are, at base, learning systems." [4]

Games have always had a major social component, and learning plays a key role in that interpersonal function. Using games to build group cohesion is an old practice, actually a triusm in team sports.

It is important to locate our peeragogical moment in a world where gaming is undergoing a renaissance. Not only has digital gaming become a large industry, but gaming has begun to infiltrate non-gaming aspects of the world, sometimes referred to as "gamification." Putting all three of these levels together, we see that we can possibly improve co-learning by adopting a playful mindset. Such a playful attitude can then mobilize any or all of the above advantages. For example,

- Two friends are learning the Russian language together. They invent a vocabulary game: one identifies an object in the world, and the other must name it in Russian. They take turns, each challenging the other, building up their common knowledge.

- A middle-aged man decides to take up hiking. The prospect is somewhat daunting, since he's a very proud person and is easily stymied by learning something from scratch. So he adopts a "trail name", a playful pseudonym. This new identity lets him set-aside his self-importance and risk making mistakes. Gradually he grows comfortable with what his new persona learns.

- We can also consider the **design** field as a useful kind of playful peeragogy. The person *playing the role* of the designer can select the contextual frame within which the design is performed. This frame can be seen as the *rules* governing the design, the artifact and the process. These rules, as with some games, may change over time. Therefore the possibility to adapt, to tailor one's activities to changing context is important when designing playful learning activities. (And we'll look at some ways to design peer learning experiences next!)

Of courbelowse, "game-based learning" can be part of standard pedagogy too. When peers create the game themselves, this presumably involves both game-based learning and peer learning. Classic strategy games like Go and CHESS also provide clear examples of peer learning practices: the question is partly, what skills and mindsets do our game-related practices really teach?

> **Plato's** Republic: "No compulsory learning can remain in the soul . . . In teaching children, train them by a kind of game, and you will be able to see more clearly the natural bent of each." (quoted by Thomas Malone)

Exercises to help cultivate a playful attitude

- Use the OBLIQUE STRATEGIES card deck (Brian Eno and Peter Schmidt, 1st edition 1975, now available in its fifth edition) to spur playful creativity. Each card advises players to change their creative process, often in surprising directions.

- Take turns making and sharing videos. This online collaborative continuous video storytelling involves a group of people creating short videos, uploading them to YouTube, then making playlists of results. Similar to CLIP KINO, only online.

- Engage in theater play using Google+ Hangout. e.g. coming together with a group of people online and performing theatrical performances on a shared topic that are recorded.

References

1. Gee, J. P. (1992). *The social mind: Language, ideology, and social practice.* Series in language and ideology. New York: Bergin & Garvey.

2. Boal, A. (1979). *Theatre of the oppressed.* 3rd ed. London: Pluto Press.

3. Bereiter, C. and Scadamalia, M. (1993). *Surpassing ourselves, an inquiry into the nature and implications of expertise.* Peru, Illinois: Open Court.

4. Douglas Thomas and John Seely Brown (2011), *A New Culture of Learning: Cultivating the Imagination for a World of Constant Change.* CreateSpace.

CHAPTER 12

K-12 PEERAGOGY

Author: Verena Roberts @verenanz *Editor*: Alison Seaman @alisonseaman

Summary

Teachers have a reputation of working in isolation, of keeping their learning to themselves and on their own islands. They are also known for generously sharing resources with one another. It is this latter trait that is becoming increasingly important as the role of the educator continues to expand. As educational technology research specialist Stephen Downes OBSERVES, the expectations on teachers have grown from "being expert in the discipline of teaching and pedagogy...[to needing to have] up-to-date and relevant knowledge and experience in it. Even a teacher of basic disciplines such as science, history or mathematics must remain grounded, as no discipline has remained stable for very long, and all disciplines require a deeper insight in order to be taught effectively." It is no longer possible for an educator to work alone to fulfil each of these roles: the solution is to work and learn in collaboration with others. This is where peer-based sharing and learning online, connected/networked learning, or peeragogy, can play an important role in helping educators.

Becoming a connected/networked learner

The following steps are set out in 'phases' in order to suggest possible experiences one may encounter when becoming connected. It is acknowledged that every learner is different and these 'phases' only serve as a guide.

Phase 1: Taking the plunge

To help educators begin to connect, the CONNECTED EDUCATOR'S STARTER KIT was created during Connected Educator's Month in August 2012. In the kit, educators will learn the distinction between connected 'educator' and connecter 'learner.' The kit also outlines wide range of Web 2.0 tools like, Twitter, Facebook, wikis, blogs and social networking to help support the educator-learner through the phases of connected learning.

The key to becoming a successful 'connected educator-learner' involves spending the time needed to learn how to learn and share in an open, connected environment. Each stage, tool and community has a learning curve and nuances of its own. In order to successfully complete each phase, connected educator-learners will need to reach out and ask for support from other learners they encounter. In turn, these new connected educator-learners will need to reciprocate by sharing learning openly. Not only will it support others' learning but it helps to foster the conditions necessary for a healthy online learning community.

Phase 2: Lurking

We all begin as lurkers. A learner can be considered a true 'lurker' after reviewing the starter kit, establishing a digital presence (through a blog or a wiki) or signing up for Twitter and creating a basic profile containing a photo. In this phase, lurkers will begin to 'FOLLOW' OTHER USERS ON TWITTER and observe EDUCATIONAL TWITTER 'CHATS'. Lurkers will also begin to seek out other resources through BLOGS, FACEBOOK, EDMODO and LINKEDIN groups.

Phase 3: Entering the fray

The lurker begins to develop into a connected educator-learner once he or she makes the decision to enter into a dialogue with another user. This could take the form of a personal blog post, participation on an education-related BLOG or WIKI or a an exchange with another Twitter user. Once this exchange takes place, relationships may begin to form and the work towards building a Personal Learning Network (PLN) begins.

One such site where such relationships can be built is CLASSROOM 2.0, which was founded by STEVE HARGADON. Through Classroom 2.0, Steve facilitates a number of free online learning opportunities including weekly BLACKBOARD COLLABORATE sessions, conferences, book projects and grassroots cross-country educational-transformation tours. Classroom 2.0 also offers a supportive Social Ning—a free, social learning space that provides online conferences and synchronous and recorded interviews with inspirational educators—for connected educator-learners around the world.

Phase 4: Building and shaping your PLN

Just as not every person one meets becomes a friend, it is important to remember that not every exchange will lead to a co-learning peeragogy arrangement. It may be sufficient to follow another who provides useful content without expecting any reciprocation. It is dependent on each educator-learner to determine who to pay attention to and what learning purpose that individual or group will serve. It is also up to the learner-educator to demonstrate to others that he or she will actively participate.

There are a number of STRATEGIES one can use when shaping the PLN to learn. However, one of the best ways educators can attract a core of *peeragogues* is by sharing actively and demonstrating active and open learning for others.

There are a number of sites where a new educator-learner can actively and openly learn. In addition to personal blogging and wikis, other professional development opportunities include open, online courses and weekly synchronous online meetings through video, podcasts or other forms of media. Examples of these opportunities are: CONNECTED LEARNING TV, TECHTALKTUESDAYS, VOLUNTEERSNEEDED, SIMPLEK12, K12 ONLINE, CEET, and EDTECHTALK. Alternatively, courses are offered with P2PU's School of Education or a wide variety of other opportunities collected by TEACHTHOUGHT and Educator's CPD online. Peggy George, the co-facilitator of the weekly Classroom 2.0 LIVE Sessions, created a livebinder package of free 'PD ON DEMAND' connected professional development online options for peeragogy enthusiasts.

Stage 5: Extending the digital PLN and connecting face-to-face

Over time, once the connected educator-learner has established a refined PLN, these peeragogues may choose to shift their learning into physical learning spaces. Some options available for these educator-learners would include the new 'grassRoots unconferences', which include examples such as: EDUCON, EDCAMPS, THATCAMP and CONNECTEDCA. These conferences are free or extremely low-cost and focus on learning from and with others. These 'unconferences' are typically publicized through Twitter, Google Apps, and Facebook. Connecting face-to-face with other peeragogues can strengthen bonds to learning networks and help to promote their sustainability.

Building personal capacity for Education 2.0

Given the large number of roles now expected of connected educators, through peeragogy, K–12 educators can now each distribute the load of the learning among networks. Although learning to connect takes time and practice, a support network is a natural accompaniment of relationship-building and open learning. Numerous online sites and social platforms exist for K–12 educators to connect and learn together as peeragogues; though the ways in which connections develop are unique. It is up to each educator to discover a passion and share it with others!

Postscript

Sylvia Tolisano, Rodd Lucier and Zoe Branigan-Pipen co-created the infographic below, which explores experiences individuals may encounter in the journey to become connected learners. It is not only a helpful entry point for new learner-educators seeking to become peeragogues, but it also serves as a wonderful example of peeragogy at work.

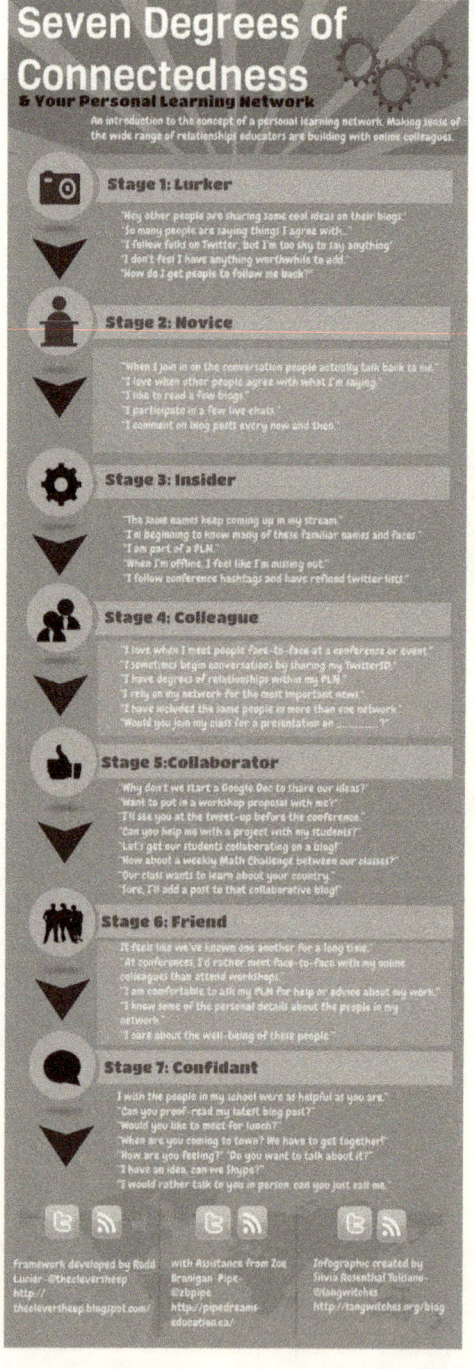

(licensed as CC By-NC-SA, on FLICKR)

Consider taking the plunge into the different stages of a Networked/Connected Educator today.

Additional resources

amazing technology tools for your classroom:

- RICHARD BYRNE
- SYLVIA TOLISANO
- CAITLIN TUCKER
- VICKI DAVIS

How to develop your PLN:

- DEGREES OF CONNECTED TEACHING by Rodd Lucier
- TEACHTHOUGHT

Theory & philosophy of connnected learning for classroom transformation:

- DAVID TRUSS
- STEVEN DOWNES
- WILL RICHARDSON

Part VI

Organizing a Learning Context

CHAPTER 13

INTRODUCTION TO ORGANIZING CO-LEARNING

This section about organizing Co-Learning rests on the assumption that learning always happens in a context, whether this context is a structured "course" or a (potentially) less structured "learning space". For the moment we consider the following division:

- *Organizing Co-learning Contexts*

    - Courses (= "learning linked to a timeline or syllabus")
    - Spaces (= "learning not necessarily linked to a timeline or syllabus")

This section focuses on existing learning contexts and examines in detail how they have been "organized" by their (co-)creators. (See also: THE STRUCTURAL DIMENSIONS OF GROUP FORMATION.)

At a "meta-level" of media, we can talk about this parallel structure:

- *Building Co-learning Platforms*

    - Development trajectories (e.g. "design, implement, test, repeat")
    - Platform features (e.g. forums, wikis, ownership models, etc.)

A given learning environment with have both time-like and space-like features as well as both designed-for and un-planned features. A given learning platform will encourage certain types of engagement and impose certain constraints. The question for both "teachers" and "system designers" – as well as for learners – should be: *what features best support learning?*

The answer will depend on the learning task and available resources.

For example, nearly everyone agrees that the best way to learn a foreign language is through immersion. But not everyone who wants to learn, say, French, can afford to drop everything to go live in a French-speaking country. Thus, the space-like full immersion "treatment" is frequently sacrificed for course-like treatments (either via books, CDs, videos, or ongoing participation in semi-immersive discussion groups).

System designers are also faced with scarce resources: programmer time, software licensing concerns, availability of peer support, and so forth. While the ideal platform would (magically) come with solutions pre-built, a more realistic approach recognizes that problem solving always takes time and energy. The problem solving approach and associated "learning orientation" will also depend on the task and resources at hand. The following sections will develop this issue further through some specific case studies.

Case study 1 (pilot, completed): "Paragogy" and the After Action Review.

In our analysis of our experiences as course organizers at P2PU, we (Joe Corneli and Charlie Danoff) used the US Army's technique of After Action Review (AAR). To quote from OUR PAPER [2]:

> As the name indicates, the AAR is used to review training exercises. It is important to note that while one person typically plays the role of evaluator in such a review [...] the review itself happens among peers, and examines the operations of the unit as a whole.
>
> The four steps in an AAR are:
>
> 1. Review what was supposed to happen (training plans).

2. Establish what happened.
3. Determine what was right or wrong with what happened.
4. Determine how the task should be done differently the next time.

> The stated purpose of the AAR is to "identify strengths and shortcomings in unit planning, preparation, and execution, and guide leaders to accept responsibility for shortcomings and produce a fix."

We combined the AAR with several principles (see Discussion section below), which we felt described effective peer learning, and went through steps 1-4 for each principle to look at how well it was implemented at P2PU. This process helped generate a range of advice that could be applied at P2PU or similar institutions. By presenteding our paper at the Open Knowledge Conference (OKCon), we were able to meet P2PU's executive director, Philipp Schmidt, as well as other highly-involved P2PU participants; our feedback may have contributed to shaping the development trajectory for P2PU.

In addition, we developed a strong prototype for constructive engagement with peer learning that we and others could deploy again. In other words, variants on the AAR and the paragogical principles could be incorporated into future learning contexts as platform features [3] or re-used in a design/administration/moderation approach [4]. For example, we also used the AAR to help structure our writing and subsequent work on paragogy.net.

Case Study 2 (in progress): "Peeragogy".

Our particular focus in the interviews was on drawing out and emphasizing the relational dimension of students, learning experiences within their environment and, consequently, on inferring from their accounts a sense of how they perceived and indeed constituted their environment. We asked them who they learned with and from and how. A further question specifically focused on whom they regarded as their peers and how they understood their peers as a source and a site for learning." [1]

In this section, we will interview and/or survey members of the Peeragogy community with questions similar to those used by Boud and Lee [1] and then identify strengths and shortcomings as we did with the AAR above. These questions are derived from the AAR.

Questions (discussed on an ETHERPAD; revisions to the original set of questions are marked in italics):

1. Who have you learned with *or* from in the Peeragogy project? *What are you doing to contribute to your peers' learning?*

2. How have you been learning during the project?

3. Who are your peers in this community, and why?

4. What were your expectations of participation in this project? *And, specifically, what did you (or do you) hope to learn through participation in this project?*

5. What actually happened during your participation in this project (so far)? *Have you been making progress on your learning goals (if any; see prev. question) – or learned anything unexpected, but interesting?*

6. What is right or wrong with what happened (Alternatively: how would you assess the project to date?)

7. How might the task be done differently next time? (What's "missing" here that would create a "next time", "sequel", or "continuation"?)

8. *How would you like to use the Peeragogy handbook?*

9. *Finally, how might we change the questions, above, if we wanted to apply them in your peeragogical context?*

Organizing Co-Learning

Reflections on participants' answers

The questions were intended to help participants reflect on, and change, their practice (i.e. their style of participation). There is a tension, however, between changing midstream and learning what we might do differently next time. There is a related tension between initial structure and figuring things out as we go. Arguably, if we knew, 100%, how to do peeragogy, then we would not learn very much in writing this handbook. Difficulties and tensions would be resolved "in advance" (see earlier comments about "magical" technologies for peer production).

And yet, despite our considerable collected expertise on collaboration, learning, and teaching, there have been a variety of tensions here! Perhaps we should judge our "success" partly on how well we deal with those. Some of the tensions highlighted in the answers are as follows:

1. *Slow formation of "peer" relationships.* There is a certain irony here: we are studying "peeragogy" and yet many respondents did not feel they were really getting to know one another "as peers", at least not yet. Those who did have a "team" or who knew one another from previous experiences, felt more peer-like in those relationships. Several remarked that they learned less from other individual participants and more from "the collective" or "from everyone". At the same time, some respondents had ambiguous feelings about naming individuals in the first question: "I felt like I was going to leave people out and that that means they would get a bad grade - ha!" One criterion for being a peer was to have built something together, so by this criterion, it stands to reason that we would only slowly become peers through this project.

2. *"Co-learning", "co-teaching", "co-producing"?* One respondent wrote: "I am learning about peeragogy, but I think I'm failing [to be] a good peeragog. I remember that Howard [once] told us that the most important thing is that you should be responsible not only for your own learning but

for your peers' learning. [...] So the question is, are we learning from others by ourselves or are we [...] helping others to learn?" Another wrote: "To my surprise I realized I could contribute organizationally with reviews, etc. And that I could provide some content around PLNs and group process. Trying to be a catalyst to a sense of forward movement and esprit de corps."

3. *Weak structure at the outset, versus a more "flexible" approach.* One respondent wrote: "I definitely think I do better when presented with a framework or scaffold to use for participation or content development. [...] (But perhaps it is just that I'm used to the old way of doing things)." Yet, the same person wrote: "I am interested in [the] applicability [of pæragogy] to new models for entrepreneurship enabling less structured aggregation of participants in new undertakings, freed of the requirement or need for an entrepreneurial visionary/source/point person/proprietor." There is a sense that some confusion, particularly at the beginning, may be typical for peeragogy. With hindsight, one proposed "solution" would be to "have had a small group of people as a cadre that had met and brainstormed before the first live session [...] tasked [with] roles [and] on the same page".

4. *Technological concerns.* There were quite a variety, perhaps mainly to do with the question: how might a (different) platform handle the tension between "conversations" and "content production"? For example, will Wordpress help us "bring in" new contributors, or would it be better to use an open wiki? Another respondent noted the utility for many readers of a take-away PDF version. The site (peeragogy.org) should be "[a] place for people to share, comment, mentor and co-learn together in an ongoing fashion."

5. *Sample size.* Note that answers are still trickling in. How should we interpret the response rate? Perhaps what matters is that we are getting "enough" responses to make an

Organizing Co-Learning 121

> analysis. One respondent proposed asking questions in a more ongoing fashion, e.g., asking people who are leaving: "What made you want to quit the project?"

With regard to Points 1 and 2, we might use some "icebreaking" techniques or a "buddy system" to pair people up to work on specific projects. The project's "teams" may have been intended to do this, but commitment or buy-in at the team level was not always high (and in many cases, a "team" ended up being comprised of just one person). It does seem that as the progress has progressed, we have begun to build tools that could address Point 3: for example, the Concept Map could be developed into a process diagram that would used to "triage" a project at its outset, help project participants decide about their roles and goals. Point 4 seems to devolve to the traditional tension between the "good enough" and the "best": we have used an existing platform to move forward in an "adequate" way. And yet, some technological improvements may be needed for future projects in pæragogy. (Furthermore, note that our choice to use a CC0 license means that if other people find the content useful, they are welcome to deploy it on their own platform, if they prefer.) Finally, Point 5 is still up in the air (more answers more be coming in shortly - I think I have sent around enough reminders). Hopefully the questionnaire will be useful to the group even with a not-100% response rate! Points 4 and 5 are related, in that an ongoing questionnaire for people leaving (or joining) the project could be implemented as a fairly simple technology, which would provide feedback for site maintainers. Gathering a little information as a condition of subscribing or unsubscribing seems like a safe, light-weight, way to learn about the users (tho there is always the possibility that rather than unsubscribing, non-participating users will just filter messages from the site).

An underlying tension (or synergy?) – between learning and producing – was highlighted in our earlier work on paragogy. If we learn by producing, that is good. However, I have argued in [4] that paragogical praxis is based less on producing and more on reusing. If downstream users of this handbook find it to, indeed, be useful, we may have done enough. *For all we know, we are the "cadre" (see above) charged with determining how best to do things in "subsequent rounds"!*And, with this, we turn to a third case study, where our work so far is reapplied in an offline educational context.

Discussion

We reconsider the appropriateness of the AAR and the paragogy principles in contexts beyond P2PU, using Lisewski and Joyce as a guide to our (meta-)critique and analysis.

> *In recent years, the tools, knowledge base and discourse of the learning technology profession has been bolstered by the appearance of conceptual paradigms such as the 'five stage e-moderating model' (Salmon, 2000) and the new mantra of 'communities of practice' (Wenger, 1998). This paper will argue that, although these frameworks are useful in informing and guiding learning technology practice, there are inherent dangers in them becoming too dominant a discourse. The main focus will be on the 'five stage e-moderating model' as providing an exemplar of a discourse which is in danger of forming a 'grand narrative' (Lyotard, 1984) or totalizing explanation of how to design and deliver online training programmes.* – Lisewski and Joyce

In a sense, the more reified a pattern, the less we learn by deploying it (SEE THESE COMMENTS). If we were trying to validate the paragogy model simply by fitting feedback to it (Case Study 2), that would be an act of intellectual dishonesty. Nevertheless, the act of fitting data to this model, as a constructive and creative act, is in fact useful – and a sign that we are still learning about what makes paragogy work. Not only on a theoretical level (summed up below), but also on a technological level (see THIS PAGE).

This table seems to suggests that paragogy is less of a grand narrative and more of a patchwork collection of tricks or heuris-

Paragogical Principles...	Reflections on practice and experience suggest...
1. *Changing context as a decentered center.* [We interact by changing the space.]	*It seems we begin with weak ties, and then experience a slow formation of "peer" relationships, as we form and re-form our social context, and come to better understand our goals.*
2. *Meta-learning as a font of knowledge.* [We interact by changing what we know about ourselves.]	*We learn a lot about ourselves by interacting with others. But participants struggle to find the right way to engage: "co-learning", "co-teaching", or "co-producing"? Moreover, "People come–they stay for a while, they flourish, they build–and they go."*
3. *Peers provide feedback that would not be there otherwise.* [We interact by changing our perspective on things.]	*We begin with a weak structure at the outset but this may afford a more "flexible" approach as time goes on (see also this* HANDBOOK SECTION *which offers advice on designing activities that help create a "flexible structure").*
4. *Paragogy is distributed and non-linear.* [We interact by changing the way things connect.]	*There are a number of technological concerns, which in a large part have to do with tensions between "content production" and "conversation", and to a lesser extent critique the platforms we're using.*
5. *Realize the dream if you can, then wake up!* [We interact by changing our objectives.]	*Even with a small group, we can extract meaningful ideas about peer learning and form a strong collective effort, which moves things forward for those involved: this means work. We would not get the same results through "pure contemplation".*

tics for group work. Rather than narrativizing peer learning, paragogy itself provides a non-linear interface that we can plug into and adapt where appropriate (like we adapted our questionnaire's questions in Case Study 2). Instead of one grand narrative, we see a growing collection of "USE CASES". The more we share our practice and experience having to do with co-organizing learning or building platforms for the same, the more robust and useful paragogy will become. It may never become a "rigorous discipline"! But if not, that is OK.

References

1. Boud, D. and Lee, A. (2005). 'PEER LEARNING' AS PEDAGOGIC DISCOURSE FOR RESEARCH EDUCATION. *Studies in Higher Education*, 30(5):501–516.

2. Joseph Corneli and Charles Jeffrey Danoff, PARAGOGY, in Sebastian Hellmann, Philipp Frischmuth, Sören Auer, and Daniel Dietrich (eds.), *Proceedings of the 6th Open Knowledge Conference, Berlin, Germany, June 30 & July 1, 2011,*

3. Joseph Corneli and Alexander Mikroyannidis (2011). PERSONALISED AND PEER-SUPPORTED LEARNING: THE PEER-TO-PEER LEARNING ENVIRONMENT (P2PLE), *Digital Education Review*, 20.

4. Joseph Corneli, PARAGOGICAL PRAXIS, to appear in *E-Learning and Digital Media* (ISSN 2042-7530), Volume 9, Number 3, 2012

5. Lisewski, B., and P. Joyce (2003). Examining the Five Stage e-Moderating Model: Designed and Emergent Practice in the Learning Technology Profession, *Association for Learning Technology Journal*, 11, 55-66.

CHAPTER 14

ADDING STRUCTURE WITH ACTIVITIES

In the introduction to "Organizing a Learning Context", we remarked that a "learning space" is *only potentially* less structured than a "course". For example, a library tends to be highly structured, with quiet rooms for reading, protocols for checking out books, a cataloging and shelving system that allows people to find what they are looking for, as well as rules that deter vandalism and theft. (Digital libraries don't need to play by all the same rules, but are still structured.)

But more structure does not always lead to better learning. In a 2010 Forbes article titled, "The Classroom in 2020," George Kembel describes a future in which "Tidy lectures will be supplanted by messy real-world challenges." The Stanford School of Design, (or "d.school" – which Kemble co-founded and currently directs) is already well-known for its open collaborative spaces, abundant supply of post-it notes and markers, and improvisational brainstorm activities – almost the opposite of traditional lecture-based learning.

One "unexpected benefit" of dealing with real-world challenges is that we can change our approach as we go. This is how it works in peer learning: peers can decide on different structures not just once (say, at the beginning of a course), but throughout the duration of their time together. This way, they are never "stuck" with existing structures, whether they be messy or clean. At least... that's the ideal.

In practice, "bottlenecks" frequently arise. For example, in a digital library context, there may be bottlenecks having to do with software development, organizational resources, community good will, or access to funding – and probably all of the above. In a didactic context, it may be as simple as one person knowing something that others do not.

While we can't eliminate scarcity in one stroke, we can design activities for peer learning that are "scarcity aware" and that help us move in the direction of adaptive learning structures.

Planning Peer Learning Activities

We begin with two simple questions:

- How do we select an appropriate learning activity?
- How do we go about creating a learning activity if we don't find an existing one?

"Planning a learning activity" should mean planning an *effective* learning activity, and in particular that means something that people can and will engage with. In short, an appropriate learning activity may be one that you already do! At the very least, current activities can provide a "seed" for even more effective ones.

> *Here's a little trick to help you keep focused on things you're trying to do. Get a bunch of index cards and do this every day: 1. Sit down and write down all the things you think you need to do right then. [...] Write them as short little notes like a "to do list". 2. Then, take the first thing that you can do right now and do it. Get it done then cross it off the card. 3. Keep doing this, and if you think of something else you need to do, put it on a card. Just keep filling them up. 4. At the end of the day, go back through your card and find any unfinished things and remove any that you'll honestly never do. 5. The next day, take all the things you didn't do from the day before and copy them onto a new card, then start with #1 again.* – Zed Shaw, in the LEARN PYTHON THE HARD WAY FORUMS

But when entering unfamiliar territory, it can be difficult to know where to begin. And remember the bottlenecks mentioned above? When you run into difficulty, ask yourself: WHY IS THIS HARD? You might try adapting Zed Shaw's exercise, and make a list of

Adding structure

limiting factors, obstacles, etc., then cross off those which you can find a strategy to deal with (add an annotation as to why). For example, you might decide to overcome your lack of knowledge in some area by hiring a tutor or expert consultant, or by putting in the hours learning things the hard way (Zed would particularly approve of the latter choice). If you can't find a strategy to deal with some issue, presumably you can table it, at least for a while.

Strategic thinking like this works well for one person. What about when you're planning activities for someone else? Here you have to be careful: remember, this is peer learning, not traditional "teaching" or "curriculum design". The first rule of thumb for *peer learning* is: don't plan activities for others unless you plan to to take part as a fully engaged participant. Otherwise, it might be a peer learning activity, but it's not yours. (Perhaps your engagement is just as "designer" – that's OK. But if you don't plan to "get" as well as "give", you're not really a peer – which is perfectly OK, but you might find other reading material that will serve you better than this handbook in that case!)

In short, it would be useful to walk through the "what do you need to do" and "why is it hard" exercises from the point of view of all of the participants, keeping in mind that they will, in general, assume different roles. To the extent that you can do so, spell out what these roles are and what activities comprise them.

For example, in a mathematics learning context, you would be likely to find people...

- solving textbook-style problems
- finding and sharing new problems
- asking questions when something seems too difficult
- fixing expository material to respond to critique
- offering critique and review of proposed solutions
- offering constructive feedback to questions (e.g. hints)
- organizing material into structured collections

- working on applications to real-world problems

- doing "meta" research activities that analyse "what works" for any and all of the above

Each one of those activities may be "hard" for one reason or another. In particular, as a system the different activities tend to depend on one another. If you have people working in a "student role" but no one who can take on a "TA role", things will be more difficult for the students. As a (co-)organizer, part of *your* job is to try to make sure all of the relevant roles are covered by someone (who may in the end wear many hats).

You can further decompose each role into specific concrete activities. They might come in the form of instructions to follow: *"How to write a good critique"* or *"How to write a proof"*. They might come in the form of accessible exercises (where "accessible" depends on the person"):*"Your first geometry problem"* or "NINETY-NINE LISP PROBLEMS", etc. Depending on the features of the learning context, you may be able to support the written instructions or exercises with live/in-person feedback (e.g. meta-critique to coach and guide novice critics, a demonstration, etc.).

Our immediate scenario: building activities for the Peeragogy Handbook

Adding a bunch of activities to the handbook won't solve all of our usability issues, but we've agreed that they will help a lot. So at this point, we are revisiting the TABLE OF CONTENTS and thinking about each article or section from this perspective:

1. When looking at this piece of text, what type of knowledge are we (and the reader) trying to gain? Technical skills (like learning how to edit Final Cut Pro), or abstract skills (like learning how to make sense of data)? What's the takeaway? I.e., what's the point?

2. What's difficult here? What might be difficult for someone else?

3. What learning activity recipes might be appropriate? (See below.)

4. What customizations do we need for this particular application?

As a quick example: designing a learning activity for the current page

1. We want to be able to come up with effective learning activities to accompany a "how to" article for peer learners. These activities will extend the "how to" aspect from the written word to the world of action.

2. It might be difficult for some of us to "unplug" from all the reading and writing that we're now habituated to doing. But peer learning isn't just about the exchange of text: there are lots and lots of ways to learn.

3. Like Neo (in one of our use cases), it could be useful to "become more aware of the peer learning we do every day". And to think about "How do you learn best?"

4. So, the proposed handbook activity is to step away from the handbook for a while. In fact, why not take a MEDIA FAST for a given period of time and look at peer learning as a basic human activity. (Hey, it just sounds to me like you might need to unplug, man!)

Resources for identifying a dozen or so "Learning Activity Recipes":

- KS TOOLKIT

- DESIGNING EFFECTIVE AND INNOVATIVE SOURCES (See the section on "Teaching Strategies for Actively Engaging Students in the Classroom")

- Each of our PATTERNS AND HEURISTICS suggest various activities, like "practicing the heuristics", "finding examples of the patterns", etc.

- Our USE CASES provide many hypothetical examples of "peeragogy in action".

Recommended Reading

THE D.SCHOOL BOOTCAMP BOOTLEG (CC-By-NC-SA) includes lots of fun activities to try. Can you crack the code and define new ones that are equally cool?

CHAPTER 15

THE STUDENT AUTHORED SYLLABUS

Authored By Suz Burroughs

In either formal learning, informal learning or models which transition between the two, there are many opportunities for learners to co-create the syllabus and/or outline their own course of action. The *sage on the stage* of formal instruction must become at the most *a guide on the side* who acts as a coach appearing only when needed rather than as a lecturer who determines the content that the learners need to master. In the following inspirational but certainly not prescriptive examples, we will focus on co-learning methods drawn from a Social Constructivist perspective, which fits nicely here.

We offer a few examples below to show a range of learner centered approaches. They all are based on co-learners hosting each other for one of a number of digestible topics in the larger subject area or domain that the group formed in order to explore. This can take place across a number of media and timelines.

The following methods will result in each co-learner gaining deep knowledge in a specific topic and moderate knowledge across several topics. The unique joy of this approach is that no two cohorts will ever be the same. The content will always be fresh, relevant, and changing. A group can even reconvene with slightly or dramatically different topics over and over using the same underlying process.

The appropriateness of the learner-created syllabus technique depends on two factors: 1) the involvement of experts in the group and 2) the level of proficiency of the group. In general, novices who may or may not have a deep interest in the subject matter benefit from more structure and experts who point to key concepts and texts. An example of this is the university survey course for first or second year students who, we assume, need more guidance as they enter the subject matter. Graduate seminars are generally much more fluid, open dialogues between motivated experts require little structure or guidance.

We also need effective methods for groups which contain novices, experts, and everyone in between. In groups with a wide range of expertise, it is important that each co-learner chooses to focus their deep inquiry on a topic that they are less familiar with. This will *even out* the expertise level across the cohort as well as ensure that a co-learner is neither bored nor dominating the dialogue.

3 example designs to structure the learning

Weekly topics structure

One way to structure the course is to have each co-learner host a topic each week. Perhaps multiple students host their topics in the same week. This progression provides a rotation of presentations and activities to support the entire group in engaging with the topics and challenges to the thinking of the presenters in a constructive and respectful manner.

Pro: co-learners have discrete timelines and manageable chunks of responsibility.

Con: the format may become disjointed, and the depth of inquiry will likely be somewhat shallow.

Milestone based structure

In this structure, each co-learner host their topics in parallel with similar activities and milestones that the whole group moves through together. Milestones can be set for a certain date, or the group can *unlock* their next milestone whenever all participants have completed the previous milestone. This second milestone timeline can be great for informal groups where participation levels may vary from week to week due to external factors, and the sense of responsibility and game-like levels can be motivating for many co-learners.

Each co-learner may start with a post of less than 500 words introducing the topic on a superficial level. When everyone has done this, the group might move on to posting questions to the post authors. Then, there may be a summary post of the activity so far with critical recommendations or insights.

Pro: co- learners have more time to digest a topic, formulate a complex schema, and generate deeper questions.

Con: it will be a few weeks before the topic level schema can form into a broader understanding of the subject matter or domain (seeing the big picture takes longer).

Relay learning structure.

This is similar to the milestone structure. However, co-learners rotate topics. If one learner posts an introductory write-up on a topic the first cycle, they may be researching questions on another topic in the next cycle, posting a summary in a third, and then posting a summary on their original topic in the fourth.

Pro: co-learners can experience responsibility for several topics.

Con: co-learners may receive a topic that is poorly researched or otherwise neglected.

Content

A vast number of topics

Within a subject of mutual interest to a group, there are a considerable number of topics or questions. What is important is that each co-learner can take responsibility for a reasonably narrow area given the duration of the course or the timeline of the group. Areas that are too broad will result in a very superficial understanding, and areas that are too narrow will result in a dull experience. For example, in marine biology, topics such as "the inter-tidal zone" may be too broad for a course cycle of a few weeks. Narrowing to one species may be too specific for a course over a few months.

Learner generated topics

Most cohorts will have some knowledge of the shared area of interest or an adjacent area. It is a good idea to respect the knowledge and experience that each member of the group brings to the table. A facilitator or coordinator may generate a list of potential topic areas, setting an example of the scale of a topic. We suggest that the participants in the group are also polled for additions to the list. In large courses, sending out a Google Form via email can be an effective way to get a quick list with a high response rate.

Expert informed topics

If there is no expert facilitator in the group, we suggest that the cohort begin their journey with a few interviews of experts to uncover what the main buzz words and areas of focus might be. One way to locate this type of expert help is through contacting authors in the subject matter on social networks, reviewing their posts for relevance, and reaching out with the request.

We recommend two people interview the expert over video chat, for example in a Hangout. One person conducts the interview, and one person takes notes and watches the time. We strongly suggest that the interview be outlined ahead of time:

Warm up: Who are you, what are your goals, and why do you think this interview will help?

Foundational questions: Ask a few questions that might elicit shortt answers to build rapport and get your interviewee talking.

Inquiry: What people say and what they do can often be very different. Ask about topics required for mastery of the subject matter (e.g. What are the areas someone would need to know about to be considered proficient in this subject?). Also, ask QUESTIONS THAT REQUIRE STORYTELLING. Avoid SUPERLATIVE or CLOSE-ENDED QUESTIONS.

Wrap up: Thank the interviewee for their time, and be sure to follow up by letting them know both what you learned and what you accomplished because they helped you.

Shared goals and group norms

Choosing useful outputs

Getting together for the sake of sharing what you know in an informal way can be fairly straightforward and somewhat useful. Most groups find that a common purpose and output that are explicitly defined and documented help to engage, motivate, and drive the group. For the examples above, the group may decide to create a blog with posts on the various topics or create a wiki where they can share their insights. Other outputs can include community service projects, business proposals, recommendations to senior management or administration, new products, and more. The key is to go beyond sharing for sharing sake and move toward an output that will be of use beyond the co-learning group. This activity is best described in CONNECTIVIST theory as the special case of networked learning where we find evidence of learning in collective action and/or behavioral change in groups rather than a psychological or neurological process in individuals.

Group cohesion (a.k.a. the rules of the road)

One challenge of this kind of collaboration is that each group will need to decide on norms, acceptable practices and behaviors. Culturally diverse groups in particular may run into communication or other issues unless there is a way to create shared expectations and communicate preferences.

One way to do this is with a team charter. This is a living document where the initial rules of engagement can live for reference. The group may add or edit this document over time based on experience, and that is a welcome thing! This documentation is a huge asset for new members joining the group who want to contribute quickly and effectively. Any co-editing word processing program will work, but we strongly recommend something that can be edited simultaneously and that lives in the cloud. (Google Docs is convenient because you can also embed your Charter into another site.)

Try starting with the following three sections, and allow some time for the group to co-edit and negotiate the document between icebreakers and kicking off the official learning process.

Mission: Why are you forming the group? What do you want to accomplish together?

Norms: Use NETIQUETTE? No FLAMING? Post your vacation days to a SHARED CALENDAR? Cultural norms?

*Members:*It is useful to include a photo and a link to a public profile such as Twitter, Google+ or Facebook.

Assessments and feedback loops

Co-authored assessment rubrics

Tests. Quizzes. Exams. How can the co-learning group assess their performance?

These types of courses benefit from an approach similar to coaching. Set goals as individuals and a group in the beginning, define what success looks like, outline steps that are needed to achieve the goal, check in on the goal progress periodically, and assess the results at the end of the course against the goal criteria. Goals may include domain expertise, a business outcome, a paper demonstrating mastery, a co-created resource, or even the quality of collaboration and adherence to shared group norms.

Learner created assessments

Another effective way to create an assessment is to decide on an individual or group output and create a peer assessment rubric based on the goals of the individual or group.

One way to create a rubric is to spend some time defining the qualities you want your output to have based on positive examples. Perhaps a group wants to create a blog. Each person on the team may identify the qualities of a great blog post based on examples that they admire. They can use that example to create a criteria for assessment of co-learner authored blog posts. We recommend that the criteria have a 0 to 5 point scale with 0 being non-existent and 5 being superb. Writing a few indicators in the 1, 3, and 5 columns helps to calibrate reviewers.

Create a SHARED DOCUMENT, perhaps starting with a list of criteria. Collapse similar criteria into one item, and create the indicators or definitions of 1, 3, and 5 point performance. Agree on the rubric, and decide on how the co-learners will be assigned assessment duties. WIll everyone review at least two others? Will each co-learner product need at least 3 reviewers before it goes live? Will you use a SPREADSHEET or a FORM to collect the assessments?

In a university setting, the instructor of record may wish to approve a peer assessment rubric, and it is sometimes a good idea to have a few outside experts give feedback on criteria that the group may have missed.

Outside assessments

It is possible that an instructor of record or similar authority will create the assessment for performance. In these cases, it is crucial that the co-learners have access to the grading rubric ahead of time so that they can ensure their activities and timeline will meet any requirements. In this case, it may be possible to require that the co-learners self-organize entirely, or there may be intermediary assignments such as the charter, project plan or literary review.

Cyclical use of these models

So much more to learn

As mentioned above, the joy of this type of learning is that no two groups will ever do it the same. Their process, goals, and outcomes can all be unique. As designers and facilitators of this type of learning environment, we can say it is a wild ride! Each class is exciting, refreshing, and on trend. The co-learners become our teachers.

If a group generates more topics than it is possible to cover at one time given the number of group members or if a group has plans to continue indefinitely, it is always possible to set up a system where potential topics are collected at all times. These unexplored topics can be harvested for use in another learning cycle, continuing until the group achieves comprehensive mastery.

Risks

This format is not without its own unique pitfalls: some challenges are learner disorientation or frustration in a new learning structure with ambiguous expectations and uneven participation. Some groups simply never gel, and we do not know why they have failed to achieve the cohesion required to move forward. Other groups are the exact opposite. Here are a few risks to consider if you would like to try the methods suggested here and how to mitigate them.

Uneven expertise: Ask co-learners to be responsible for topics that are new to them.

Uneven participation and cohesion: Ask co-learners what they want to do to motivate the group rather than imposing your own ideas.

Experts/facilitators that kill the conversation: In the charter or other documentation, explicitly state that the purpose of the discussion is to further the conversation, and encourage experts to allow others to explore their own thinking by asking probing (not leading) questions.

Ambiguous goals: Encourage the group to document their mission and what they will do as a team. This can change over time, but it is best to start out with a clear purpose.

Conclusion

Make mistakes. Correct course. Invite new perspectives. Create a structure that everyone can work with. Change it when it breaks. Most of all, have fun!

CHAPTER 16

CONNECTIVISM IN PRACTICE — HOW TO ORGANIZE A MOOC

Massive Open Online Courses (MOOCs) are online learning events that can take place synchronously and asynchronously for months. Participants assemble to hear, see, and participate in backchannel communication during live lectures. They read the same texts at the same time, according to a calendar. Learning takes place through self-organized networks of participants, and is almost completely decentralized: individuals and groups create blogs or wikis around their own interpretations of the texts and lectures, and comment on each other's work; each individual and group publicises their RSS feed, which are automatically aggregated by a special (freely available) tool, gRSShopper. Every day, an email goes out to all participants, aggregating activity streams from all the blogs and wikis that engage that week's material. MOOCs are a practical application of a learning theory known as "connectivism" that situates learning in the networks of connections made between individuals and between texts.

Not all MOOCs are Connectivist MOOCs (sometimes called **cMOOCs**). Platforms such as Coursera, edX and Udacity are famously offering MOOCs which follow a more traditional, centralized approach (sometimes called **xMOOCs**). In those xMOOCs a professor is taking the lead and the learning-experience is organized top-down. However, some xMOOCs seem to adopt a more blended approach. For instance, the course E-learning and Digital Cultures will make use of online spaces beyond the Coursera environment, and they want some aspects of participation in this course to involve the wider social web.

In this chapter we'll focus on cMOOCs. One might wonder why a course would want to be 'massive' and what '**massive**' means. cMOOC-pioneer Stephen Downes explains that his focus is on the development of a network structure, as opposed to a group structure, to manage the course. In a network structure there isn't any central focus, for example, a central discussion. That's also the reason why he considers the figure of 150 (active participants), **Dunbar's Number**, as the cut-off line in order to talk about 'massive':

> Why Dunbar's number? The reason is that it represents the maximum (theoretical) number of people a person can reasonably interact with. How many blogs can a person read, follow and respond to? Maybe around 150, if Dunbar is correct. Which means that if we have 170 blogs, then the blogs don't constitute a 'core' - people begin to be selective about which blogs they're reading, and different (and interacting) subcommunities can form.

Introduction

Traditionally, scholars distinguish between three main CATEGORIES OF LEARNING THEORIES: behaviorism, cognitivism and constructivism. Some would add a fourth one: CONNECTIVISM, but this is DISPUTED. One interesting application of connectivism, a learning theory and practice for the digital era, is the Massive Open Online Course.

A learning theory for the digital age

The connectivist theory describes learning as a process of creating connections and developing networks. It is based on the premise that knowledge exists out in the world, rather than inside an individual's mind. Connectivism sees the network as a central metaphor for learning, with a node in the network being a concept (data, feelings, images, etc.) that can be meaningfully related to other nodes. Not all connections are of equal strength in this metaphor; in fact, many connections may be quite weak.

On a practical level, this approach recommends that learning should focus on where to find information (streams), and how to evaluate and mash up those streams, rather than trying to enter lots of (perishable) information into one's skull. Knowing the pipes is more important than knowing what exactly each pipe contains at a given moment.

STEPHEN DOWNES and GEORGE SIEMENS promote the idea of connectivism. They also practice it, by organizing Massive Open Online Courses (MOOCs): for instance, CHANGE11. People are free to participate at will. Each week a subject is discussed during synchronous sessions, which are recorded and uploaded for reference on the Change11 website. The site also includes an archive of daily newsletters and RSS-feeds of blog posts and tweets from participants.

MOOCs tend to be very learner-centered. People are encouraged to pursue their own interests and link up with others who might help them. But the distributed and free nature of the projects also leads to complaints; participants often find it confusing when they attempt to follow up on all the discussions (the facilitators say one should not try to follow up on *all* the content).

Stephen Downes explains in WHAT CONNECTIVISM IS: "This implies a pedagogy that (a) seeks to describe 'successful' networks (as identified by their properties, which I have characterized as diversity, autonomy, openness, and connectivity); and (b) seeks to describe the practices that lead to such networks, both in the individual and in society (which I have characterized as modeling and demonstration (on the part of a teacher) and practice and reflection (on the part of a learner)."

George Siemens says connectivism is a "LEARNING THEORY FOR THE DIGITAL AGE."

Connectivism in practice

One example of a MOOC that claims to embody the connectivist theory is CHANGE.MOOC.ca. The "HOW IT WORKS" section of the site explains what connectivism means in practice.

The MOOC organizers developed a number of ways to combine the distributed nature of the discussions with the need for a constantly updated overview and for a federated structure. So, if your team wants to organize an open online course, these are five points to take into consideration:

There is no body of content the participants have to memorize, but the learning results from activities they undertake. The activities are different for each person. A course schedule with suggested reading, assignments for synchronous or asynchronous sessions is provided (using Google Docs spreadsheets internally, Google Calendar externally - one could also use a wiki), but participants are free to pick and choose. Normally there is a topic, activities, reading resources and often a guest speaker for each week. One should even reflect upon the question whether a start- and end date are actually needed. It is crucial to explain the particular philosophy of this kind of MOOC, and this right from the outset, because chances are learners will come with expectations informed by their more traditional learning experiences.

1. It is important to discuss the "internal" aspects, such as self-motivation: what do the participants want to achieve, what is their larger goal? And what are their intentions when they select certain activities (rather than other possibilities)? Everyone has her own intended outcome. Suggest that participants meditate on all this and jot down their objectives. And how can they avoid becoming stressed out and getting depressed because they feel they cannot "keep up with all this?" The facilitators should have a good look at these motivations, even if it's impossible to assist every participant individually (for large-scale MOOCs).

2. Ideally, participants should prepare for this course by acquiring the necessary digital skills. Which skills are "necessary" can be decided by the group itself in advance. It's all about selecting, choosing, remixing - also called "curating". There are lots of tools which you can use for this: blogs, social bookmarks, wikis, mindmaps, forums, social

dashboards, networks such as Twitter with their possibilities such as hashtags and lists. Maybe these tools are self-evident for some, but not necessarily for all the participants.

3. The course is not located in one place but is distributed across the web: on various blogs and blogging platforms, on various groups and online networks, on photo- and video-sharing platforms, on mindmaps and other visualization platforms, on various tools for synchronous sessions. This wide variety is in itself an important learning element.

4. There are weekly synchronous sessions (using Blackboard collaborate, or similar group chatting tool). During these sessions, experts and participants give presentations and enter into discussions. Groups of participants also have synchronous meetings at other venues (such as Second Life). Try to plan this well in advance!

5. Many participants highly appreciate efforts to give an overview of the proceedings. Specifically, the DAILY NEWSLETTER is a kind of hub, a community newspaper. In that Daily there is also a list of the blog posts mentioning the course-specific tag (e.g. "Change11"), also the tweets with hashtag #change11 are listed in the Daily. Of course, the MOOC has a SITE where sessions, newsletters and other resources are archived and discussion threads can be read.

From the very beginning of the course, it's necessary to explain the importance of tagging the various contributions, to suggest a hashtag.

For harvesting all this distributed content, Stephen Downes advocates the use of GRSSHOPPER, which is a personal web environment that combines resource aggregation, a personal dataspace, and personal publishing (Downes developed it and would like to build a hosted version - eventually financed via Kickstarter). The gRSShopper can be found on a registration page, which is useful primarily for sending the newsletter. It allows you to organize your online content any way you want, to import content - your own or others' - from remote sites, to remix and repurpose it, and to distribute it as RSS, web pages, JSON data, or RSS feeds. DOWNES: "For example, the gRSShopper harvester will harvest a link from a given feed. A person, if he or she has admin privileges, can transform this link into a post, adding his or her own comments. The post will contain information about the original link's author and journal. Content in gRSShopper is created and manipulated through the use of system code that allows administrators to harvest, map, and display data, as well as to link to and create their own content. gRSShopper is also intended to act as a fully-fledged publishing tool." (for alternatives, see the technologies section further on).

Alternatives for registrations: Google Groups for instance. But specific rules about privacy should be dealt with: what will be the status of the contributions? In this MOOC the status is public and open by default, for Downes this is an important element of the course.

Technologies

Some MOOCs use Moodle, but Downes dislikes the centralization aspect and it's not as open as it could be, saying "people feel better writing in their own space." Other possibilities: Google Groups, Wordpress, Diigo, Twitter, Facebook page, Second Life; but each course uses different mixtures of the many tools out there. People choose their environment - whether it is WoW or Minecraft. Students use Blogger, WordPress, Tumblr, Posterous as blogging tools.

Key element is RSS harvesting

Give participants a means to contribute their blogfeed. In "ADD A NEW FEED," Downes explains how to get this structure and additional explanations (via videos) in order to contribute their blog feed. The administrator in this case uses gRSShopper to process the content and put it in a database, process it and send it to other people. Alternatively one can use Google Reader (the list of feeds is available as an OPML file - which can be imported to other platforms). There is also a plug-in for Wordpress that lets you use a Google Doc spreadsheet for the feeds, then Wordpress for the aggregation). Many other content management systems have RSS harvesting features.

Each individual could run her own aggregator, but Downes offers it as a service. But aggregators are needed, whether individual, centralized or both.

Specialized harvesting

Using Twitter, Diigo, Delicious, Google Groups, If This Then That (IFTTT) and FEED43 (take ordinary web page and turn it into an RSS feed).

Synchronous environments

Synchronous platforms include Blackboard Collaborate (used now for Change11); Adobe Connect; Big Blue Button; WizIQ; Fuze; WebX; webcasting; web radio; videoconferencing with Skype or Google Hangout in conjunction with Livestream or ustream.tv. Or take the Skype/Hangout audiostream and broadcast is as webradio. Set up and test ahead of time, but don't hesitate to experiment.

Newsletter or Feeds

Feeds are very important (see earlier remarks about the Daily newsletter). You can use Twitter or a Facebook page, Downes uses email, also creates an RSS version through gRSShopper and sends it through Ifttt.com back to Facebook and Twitter. For the rest of us there is Wordpress, which you can use to CREATE AN EMAIL NEWS LETTER. Downs also suggests this handy guide on HOW TO DESIGN AND BUILD AN EMAIL NEWSLETTER WITHOUT LOOSING YOUR MIND!

Consider using a content management system and databases to put out specialized pages and the newsletter in an elegant way, but it requires a learning curve. Otherwise, use blogs / wikis.

Comments

Participants are strongly encouraged to comment on each others' blogs and to launch discussion threads. By doing so they practice a fundamental social media skill - developing networks by commenting on various places and engaging in conversations. It is important to have activities and get people to be involved rather than sit back.

For an in-depth presentation, please have a look at FACILITATING A MASSIVE OPEN ONLINE COURSE by Stephen Downes, in which he focuses on research and survey issues, preparing events, and other essentials.

Resources

Basics

- HOW THIS COURSE WORKS
- WHAT IS A MOOC
- SUCCESS IN A MOOC
- KNOWLEDGE IN A MOOC
- INTRODUCTION AND INVITATION

Further reading

- Downes & Siemens MOOC SITE
- WHAT CONNECTIVISM IS by Stephen Downes
- AN INTRODUCTION TO CONNECTIVE KNOWLEDGE by Stephen Downes
- FACILITATING A MASSIVE OPEN ONLINE COURSE, by Stephen Downes
- GRSSHOPPER

How to Organize a MOOC

- CONNECTIVISM: A LEARNING THEORY FOR THE DIGITAL AGE by George Siemens
- A CONNECTIVISM GLOSSARY
- RHIZOMES AND NETWORKS by George Siemens
- RHIZOMATIC EDUCATION: COMMUNITY AS CURRICULUM by Dave Cormier
- KNOWING KNOWLEDGE, a book by George Siemens
- NET SMART, Howard Rheingold (about internal and external literacies for coping with the 'always on' digital era)
- MASSIVE OPEN ONLINE COURSES: Setting Up (StartTo-MOOC, Part 1)
- LITERATURE REVIEW

Relevant Handbook pages

PERSONAL LEARNING NETWORKS

CHAPTER 17

PARTICIPATION

Methods of managing projects, including learning projects, range from more formal and structured to casual and unstructured. As a facilitator, you'll see your peeragogy community constantly adjust, as it seeks an equilibrium between order and chaos, ideally allowing everyone to be involved at their own pace without losing focus, and in such a manner that the collective can deliver.

Hey you, stop this train!

For teachers reading this, and wondering how to use peeragogy to improve participation in their classrooms, it's really quite simple: reframe the educational vision using peeragogical eyes. Recast the classroom as a community of people who learn together, the teacher as facilitator, and the curriculum as a starting point that can be used to organize and trigger community engagement. However, just because it's simple doesn't mean it's easy! Whatever your day job may be, consider: how well do the various groups you participate in work together – even when the members ostensibly share a common purpose? Sometimes things tick along nicely, and, presumably, sometimes it's excruciating. What's your role in all of this? How do *you* participate?

Guidelines for participation

- Accept that some people want to watch what is going on before jumping in. This doesn't mean you have to keep them hanging around forever. After a while, you may un-enroll people who don't add any value to the community. In our Peeragogy project, we've asked people to explicitly re-enroll several times. Most do renew; some leave.

- Accept that people may only contribute a little: if this contribution is good it will add value to the whole.

- Understand that you can not impose strict deadlines on volunteers; adjust targets accordingly.

- Let your work be "open" in the sense described in Wikipedia's NEUTRAL POINT OF VIEW policy.

- Give roles to participants and define some "energy centers" who will take the lead on specific items in the project.

- Organize regular face-to-face or online meetings to talk about progress and what's needed in upcoming days/weeks.

- Ask participants to be clear about when they will be ready to deliver their contributions.

- Have clear deadlines, but allow contributions that come in after the deadline – in general, be flexible.

- Add a newcomer section on your online platform to help new arrivals get started. Seasoned participants are often eager to serve as mentors.

Participation

When we think about project management in an organization, we often relate to well-established tools and processes. For example, we will use the PROJECT MANAGEMENT BODY OF KNOWLEDGE (PMBOK) as a standard. For the Project Management Institute (PMI) and most workers, those standards are the key to project success. In classical project management, tasks and deadlines are clearly defined. We will, for example, use PROGRAM EVALUATION AND REVIEW TECHNIC (PERT) to analyze and represent tasks. We often represent the project schedule using a GANTT CHART. Those are just two of the project management tools that illustrate how project management rests firmly on its engineering background. In those very structured projects, each actor is expected to work exactly as planned and to deliver his part of the work on time; every individual delay potentially leading to a collective delay.

Peeragogy projects often expect to break the 90/9/1 RULE, with everyone participating, not just a few. Once again, some participants may not contribute often – but one really good idea is actually a major contribution. See MISUNDERSTANDING POWER for some further reflections on these matters.

CHAPTER 18

THE WORKSCAPE, A LEARNING PLATFORM FOR CORPORATIONS

Summary

Cultivating a results-oriented peer-learning program in a corporate learning ecosystem involves a few tweaks of the approach and tools we discussed in relation to more open, diverse networks.

JAY CROSS *talks about* WORKSCAPES *on* VIMEO.

The Workscape, a platform for learning

Formal learning takes place in classrooms; informal learning happens in *workscapes.* A workscape is a learning ecology. As the environment of learning, a workscape includes the workplace. In fact, a workscape has no boundaries. No two workscapes are alike. Your workscape may include being coached on giving effective presentations, calling the help desk for an explanation, and researching an industry on the Net. My workscape could include participating in a community of field technicians, looking things up on a search engine, and living in France for three months. Developing a platform to support informal learning is analogous to landscaping a garden. A major component of informal learning is natural learning, the notion of treating people as organisms in nature. The people are free-range learners. Our role is to protect their environment, provide nutrients for growth, and let nature take its course. A landscape designer's goal is to conceptualize a harmonious, unified, pleasing garden that makes the most of the site at hand. A workscape designer's goal is to create a learning environment that increases the organization's longevity and health and the individual's happiness and well-being. Gardeners don't control plants; managers don't control people. Gardeners and managers have influence but not absolute authority. They can't makea plant fit into the landscape or a person fit into a team. In an ideal Workscape, workers can easily find the people and information they need, learning is fluid and new ideas flow freely, corporate citizens live and work by the organization's values, people know the best way to get things done, workers spend more time creating value than handling exceptions, and everyone finds their work challenging and fulfilling.

The technical infrastructure of the Workscape

When an organization is improving its Workscape, looking at consumer applications is a good way to think about what's required. Ask net-savvy younger workers how they would like to learn new skills, and they bring up the features they enjoy in other services:

- Personalize my experience and make recommendations, like Amazon

- Make it easy for me to connect with friends, like Facebook

- Keep me in touch with colleagues and associates in other companies, as on LinkedIn

- Persistent reputations, as at eBay, so you can trust who you're collaborating with

- Multiple access options, like a bank that offers access by ATM, the Web, phone, or human tellers

- Don't overload me. Let me learn from YouTube, an FAQ, or linking to an expert

- Show me what's hot, like Reddit, Digg, MetaFilter, or Fark do

- Give me single sign-on, like using my Facebook profile to access multiple applications

The Workscape

- Let me choose and subscribe to streams of information I'm interested in, like BoingBoing, LifeHacker or Huffpost.

- Provide a single, simple, all-in-one interface, like that provided by Google for search

- Help me learn from a community of kindred spirits, like SlashDot, Reddit, and MetaFilter

- Give me a way to voice my opinions and show my personality, as on my blog

- Show me what others are interested in, as with social bookmarks like Diigo and Delicious

- Make it easy to share photos and video, as on Flickr and YouTube

- Leverage "the wisdom of crowds," as when I pose a question to my followers on Twitter or Facebook

- Enable users to rate content, like "Favoriting" an item on Facebook or +!ing is on Google or YouTube

Some of those consumer applications are simple to replicate in-house. Others are not. You can't afford to replicate Facebook or Google behind your firewall. That said, there are lots of applications you can implement at reasonable cost. Be skeptical if your collaborative infrastructure that doesn't include these minimal functions:

Profiles - for locating and contacting people with the right skills and background. Profile should contain photo, position, location, email address, expertise (tagged so it's searchable). IBM's Blue Pages profiles include how to reach you (noting whether you're online now), reporting chain (boss, boss's boss, etc.), link to your blog and bookmarks, people in your network, links to documents you frequently share, members of your network.

Activity stream - for monitoring the organization pulse in real time, sharing what you're doing, being referred to useful information, asking for help, accelerating the flow of news and information, and keeping up with change

Wikis - for writing collaboratively, eliminating multiple versions of documents, keeping information out in the open, eliminating unnecessary email, and sharing responsibility for updates and error correction

Virtual meetings - to make it easy to meet online. Minimum feature set: shared screen, shared white board, text chat, video of participants. Bonus features: persistent meeting room (your office online), avatars.

Blogs - for narrating your work, maintaining your digital reputation, recording accomplishments, documenting expert knowledge, showing people what you're up to so they can help out

Bookmarks - to facilitate searching for links to information, discover what sources other people are following, locate experts

Mobile access - Half of America's workforce sometimes works away from the office. Smart phones are surpassing PCs for connecting to networks for access and participation. Phones post most Tweets than computers. Google designs its apps for mobile before porting them to PCs.

Social network - for online conversation, connecting with people, and all of the above functions.

Conclusion

Learning used to focus on what was in an individual's head. The individual took the test, got the degree, or earned the certificate. The new learning focuses on what it takes to do the job right. The workplace is an open-book exam. What worker doesn't have a cell phone and an Internet connection? Using personal information pipelines to get help from colleagues and the Internet to access the world's information is encouraged. Besides, it's probably the team that must perform, not a single individual. Thirty years ago, three-quarters of what a worker need to do the job was stored in her head; now it's less than 10%.

Part VII

Cooperation

CHAPTER 19

INTRODUCTION TO COOPERATION: CO-FACILITATION

Author: MARIA ARENAS, with contributions by CHARLIE DANOFF

Facilitation is a process of helping groups work cooperatively and effectively. Facilitation can be particularly helpful for individuals who, based on a certain level of insecurity or inexperience, tend to lurk rather than participate. At the same time, it in peeragogy, a facilitator isn't necessarily an "authority": rather, facilitation work is done in service to the group and the group dialogue and process. For example, a facilitator may simply "hold space" for the group, by setting up a meeting or a regular series of discussions.

Co-facilitating in peer-to-peer learning

Co-facilitation can be found in collaborations between two or more people who need each other to complete a task, for example, learn about a given subject, author a technical report, solve a problem, or conduct research Dr. Fink writes in *Creating Significant Learning Experiences* (Jossey Bass, 2003) that "in this process, there has to be some kind of change in the learner. No change, no learning". Significant learning requires that there be some kind of lasting change that is important in terms of the learner's life; therefore a way to measure the effectiveness of co-facilitation is if there's been a change in the peer group.

The board of a housing association needs to set a strategy that takes account of major changes in legislation, the UK benefits system and the availability of long term construction loans. Julian, eager to make use of his new-found peeragogical insights suggests an approach where individuals research specific factors and the team work together to draw out themes and strategic options. As a start he proposes that each board member researches an area of specific knowledge or interest. Jim, the Chairman, identifies questions he wants to ask the Chairs of other Housing Associations. Pamela (a lawyer) agrees to do an analysis of the relevant legislation. Clare, the CEO, plans out a series of meetings with the local councils in the boroughs of interest to understand their reactions to the changes from central government. Jenny, the operations director, starts modelling the impact on occupancy from new benefits rules. Colin, the development director, re-purposes existing work on options for development sites to reflect different housing mixes on each site. Malcolm, the finance director, prepares a briefing on the new treasury landscape and the changing positions of major lenders. Each member of the board documents their research in a private wiki. Julian facilitates some synchronous and asynchronous discussion to draw out themes in each area and map across the areas of interest. Malcolm, the FD, adapts his financial models to take different options as parameters. Clare refines the themes into a set of strategic options for the association, with associated financial modelling provided by Malcolm. Individual board members explore the options asynchronously before convening for an all-day meeting to confirm the strategy.

Which roles, competences and skills do we need to co-facilitate?

Co-facilitation roles can be found in groups/teams like basketball, health, Alcoholics Anonymous, spiritual groups, etc. For example, self-help groups are composed of people who gather to share common problems and experiences associated with a particular problem, condition, illness, or personal circumstance.

"Freedom to Learn" is among the learning theories for which CARL ROGERS was known. Commenting on Rogers' related work, Barrett-Lennard remarked: "...he offered several hypothesized general principles. These included: We cannot teach another person directly; we can only facilitate his learning. The structure and organization of the self appears to become more rigid under threat; to relax its boundaries when completely free from threat.... The educational situation which most effectively promotes significant learning is one in which 1) threat to the self of the learner is reduced a minimum, and 2) differentiated perception of the field of experience is facilitated."

Part of the facilitator's role is to create a safe place for learning to take place; but they should also challenge the participants. As John Wooden said of coaching: "Be quick, but don't hurry." JOHN HERON articulated this aspect of facilitation well:

> "Too much hierarchical control, and participants become passive and dependent or hostile and resistant. They wane in self-direction, which is the core of all learning. Too much cooperative guidance may degenerate into a subtle kind of nurturing oppression, and may deny the group the benefits of totally autonomous learning. Too much autonomy for participants and laissez-faire on your part, and they may wallow in ignorance, misconception, and chaos."

Co-facilitating discussion forums

If peers are preparing a forum discussion, here are some ideas from "The tool box", that can be helpful as guidelines for running this type of meetings:

- Explain the importance of collaborative group work and make it a requirement.

- Establish how you will communicate in the forum

- Be aware of mutual blind spots in facilitating and observing others

- Watch out for different rhythms of intervention".

Co-facilitating wiki workflows

A good place to begin for any co-facilitators working with a wiki is Wikipedia's famous "5 Pillars."

- Wikipedia is an encyclopedia

- Wikipedia writes articles from a neutral point-of-view

- Wikipedia is free content that anyone can edit, use, modify, and distribute.

- Editors should interact with each other in a respectful and civil manner.

- Wikipedia does not have firm rules.

Co-facilitating live sessions

Learning experiences in Live Sessions which include Social Media and co facilitating exercise is described in the article" Learning Re-imagined: Participatory, Peer, Global, Online" by Howard Rheingold, we have taken inspiration from his points and re-mixed them slightly.

- Establish roles for co facilitators and participants (moderator, technical recorder, writer to take notes, etc..).

- Provide a reading list – indicating what is really important and what is more "nice to know".

- Ideally before, or when the session begins, take some time to allow participants to familiarize themselves with the tools.

- Introduce yourself and your peers (co-facilitators) and ask the members to make a brief introduction of themselves.

- Review the agenda for the session, both to make sure there *is* an agenda (at the start) and to make sure everything was covered (at the end).

- Online tools like: Mumble, Diigo, Etherpad and chat can be used to communicate and interact in the session. However, consider whether participants are interested in experimenting with lots of tools. Often more tools (and some content) can end up making tasks harder.

- Keep it Simple Stupid, or KISS: Remember you came together with your peers to accomplish something not to discuss an agenda or play with online tools; keep everything as easily accessible as possible to ensure you realize your peer goals.

Paragogical Action Review

Following any co-facilitating session it is essential that the co-facilitators come together and review what happened. A useful framework is the Paragogical Action Review (PAR), based on the U.S. Army's AFTER ACTION REVIEW, which has four components, to which we have added a fifth. A further difference in the Paragogical Action Review is that it need not take place "after" the action, but can be integrated into the action (accordingly, we use a present tense phrasing).

- Review what was supposed to happen (training plans)
- Establish what is happening
- Determine what's right or wrong with what's happening
- Determine how the task should be done differently in the future
- Share your notes with your other peers for feedback and to improve things going forward

Here we can make use of an obvious pun: in golf, the *par* is related to the difficulty of play. If we understand the difficulties in advance, we can help participants prepare to meet them. Additionally if we reassess the difficulties and challenges as we go, we can adapt our technique to suit current needs. The key to using the PAR to effectively facilitate co-learning is replacing the "blind spot" at the center of every defensive formation with a horizon, allowing our thought process a vigorous confrontation with mystery. Instead of finding the 'unknown' at the end of a long upriver journey amidst dubious colonial and racial politics, we find it right in the heart of our mediated communications, in the form of silence.

Resources

1. PEER EDUCATION: TRAINING OF TRAINERS MANUAL; UN Interagency Group on Young Peoples Health
2. Co FACILITATING: Advantages & Potential Disadvantages. J. Willam Pfeifer and John E Johnes
3. A SUMMARY of John Heron's model on role of facilitators
4. CARL ROGERS, CORE CONDITIONS AND EDUCATION, Encyclopedia of Informal Education
5. PEER MEDIATION, Study Guides and Strategies

6. CO-FACILITATION: THE ADVANTAGES AND CHALLENGES, Canadian Union of Public Employees

7. BOHEMIA INTERACTIVE COMMUNITY WIKI GUIDELINES

8. Barrett-Lennard, G. T. (1998) *CARL ROGER'S HELPING SYSTEM. JOURNEY AND SUBSTANCE*, London: Sage

9. 5 PILLARS OF WIKIPEDIA, from Wikipedia

10. TRAINING THE FORCE, *(2002)*US Army Field Manual #FM 7-0 (FM 25-100)

11. LEARNING REIMAGINED: PARTICIPATORY, PEER, GLOBAL, ONLINE, by Howard Rheingold

12. RESEARCH GATE is a network dedicated to science and research, in which members connect, collaborate and discover scientific publications, jobs and conferences.

13. CREATING AND FACILITATING PEER SUPPORT GROUPS, by The Community Tool Box

14. FACILITATION TIPS, by Villanova University

15. HERDING PASSIONATE CATS: THE ROLE OF FACILITATOR IN A PEER LEARNING, by Pippa Buchanan

16. REFLECTIVE PEER FACILITATION: CRAFTING COLLABORATIVE SELF-ASSESSMENT, by Dale Vidmar, Southern Oregon University Library

17. EFFECTIVE CO-FACILITATION, by Everywoman's Center, University of Massachussetts

18. "TEACHING SMART PEOPLE HOW TO LEARN" by Chris Argyris, Harvard Business Review 69.3, 1991; also published in expanded form as a BOOK with the same name.

CHAPTER 20

PARAGOGICAL DESIGNS FOR CO-WORKING

Here our aim is to develop the productive "paragogical" side of peeragogy through a discussion of the strategies, joys, and sorrows of co-working. It complements the CO-FACILITATION page.

These questions could apply to our working group(s) here, and to pretty much any working group in existence:

- How do you pass the ball?

- How do you keep the energy going?

- How do you diagnose where the group is going and make things "intentional" instead of assumed?

How do we do all of this in a way that achieves shared and mutual understanding, mindfulness of process and growth, in service to a collective output, or expression, or course of action that is more than just the sum of parts? The word "learning" does not adequately capture what it means to figure out the "for what purpose or reason?" dimension that is essential for a peeragogical endeavor. Interpersonal exchange and collaboration in service to communal understanding goes further than (mere) "learning". In particular, here we will consider the role of collective knowledge exchange and synthesis towards the end of *getting things done*.

Co-working as the flip side of convening

Linus Torvalds, interviewed by Steven Vaughan-Nichols for a Hewlett-Packard publication, had this to say about software development:

> The first mistake is thinking that you can throw things out there and ask people to help. That's not how it works. You make it public, and then you assume that you'll have to do all the work, and ask people to come up with suggestions of what you should do, not what they should do. Maybe they'll start helping eventually, but you should start off with the assumption that you're going to be the one maintaining it and ready to do all the work. The other thing–and it's kind of related–that people seem to get wrong is to think that the code they write is what matters. No, even if you wrote 100% of the code, and even if you are the best programmer in the world and will never need any help with the project at all, the thing that really matters is the users of the code. The code itself is unimportant; the project is only as useful as people actually find it.

It is important to understand your users – and remember that contributors are a special class of "user" with a real time investment in the way the project works. We typically cannot "Tom Sawyer" ourselves into leisure or ease just because we manage to work collaboratively, or just because we have found people with some common interests.

The truth is probably somewhere in between Torvalds and Twain. Many people actively want to contribute! For example, on "Wikipedia, the encyclopedia anyone can edit" (as of 2011) AS MANY AS 80,000 visitors make 5 or more edits per month. This is interesting to compare with the FACT that (as of 2006) "over 50% of all the edits are done by just .7% of the users... 24 people...and in fact the most active 2%, which is 1400 people, have done 73.4% of all the edits." Similar numbers apply to other peer production communities.

'AIN'T THAT WORK?'

A little theory

In many natural systems, things are not distributed equally, and it is not atypical for e.g. 20% of the population to control 80% of the wealth (or, as we saw, for 2% of the users to do nearly 80% of the edits). Many, many systems work like this, so maybe there's a good reason for it.

Let's think about it in terms of "coordination" as thought of by the late Elinor Ostrom. She talked about "local solutions for local problems". By definition, such geographically-based coordination requires close proximity. What does "close" mean? If we think about homogeneous space, it just means that we draw a circle (or sphere) around where we are, and the radius of this circle (resp. sphere) is small. An interesting MATHEMATICAL FACT is that as the dimension grows, the volume of the sphere gets "thinner", so the radius must increase to capture the same d-dimensional volume when d grows! Based on this, we might guess that the more dimensions a problem has, the more resources we will need to solve it. From another perspective, the more different factors impact a given issue, in some sense, the less likely there are to be small scale, self-contained, "local problems" in the first place.

If we think about networks instead of homogeneous space, and notice that some nodes in the network have more connections than others, then we see the same issue applies to these nodes: they have more complexity in their immediate region than the others. This might suggest that such "central nodes" (e.g. popular films, popular words, popular websites, popular people) would, by definition, be less discriminating in terms of who/what they couple with. On a certain level (weak ties) this is probably true. But on another level (strong ties) I think it must not be true – you can't really have it both ways.

Asking for organizations to work on the "local" level of strong ties when they are "really" all about many low-bandwidth weak ties isn't likely to work well. Google is happy to serve everyone's web requests – but they can't have just anyone walking in off the street and connecting devices their network in Mountain View. (Aside: the 2006 article on Wikipedia quoted above was written by Aaron Swartz, who achieved some NOTORIETY for doing essentially just that, though in his case, it was MIT's network, not Google's.) We might guess that the more institutionally committed someone is, the less likely they are to be able to form deep connections with anyone who is not an integral part of their institution.

Of course, we don't "give up". We aspire to create systems that have both aspects, systems where a "dedicated individual can rise to the top through dint of effort", etc. These systems are well articulated, almost like natural languages, which are so expressive and adaptive that "most sentences have never been said before". In other words, a well-articulated system does lend itself to "local solutions to local problems" – but only because all words are NOT created equal.

My brothers read a little bit. Little words like 'If' and 'It.' My father can read big words, too, Like CONSTANTINOPLE and TIMBUKTU.

Co-working: what is an institution?

We could talk in this section about Coase's theory of the firm, and Benkler's theory of "Coase's Penguin". We might continue QUOTING from Aaron Swartz. But we will not get so deep into that here: you can explore it on your own!

CHAPTER 21

DESIGNING A PLATFORM FOR PEER LEARNING

Author: Joe Corneli

PLANETMATH is *a virtual community which aims to help make mathematical knowledge more accessible.* This article summarizes the main design ideas behind a complete rebuild of the site's platform. It gets a little technical, but don't worry, there's not too much *math* here...

In short: I lumped the different activities that people could do on PlanetMath.org into 5 categories (see the table below). More or less this table just means that on PlanetMath, people write articles and link these articles to other articles, add comments, ask questions, make corrections, and connect problems and solutions to expository material. They also deploy HEURISTICS for solving problems – and they MAKE AND JOIN GROUPS.

The five categories (Context, Engagement, Quality, Structure, and Heuristic) come from reflecting on the 5 PARAGOGY PRINCIPLES, and comparing them with the Martin Nowak's 5 RULES FOR THE EVOLUTION OF COOPERATION, then clustering the actual activities that people can do on PlanetMath (as well as some new planned activities) into these categories. I also drew inspiration from the pattern and heuristic "language" we developed in the

Context	Feedback	Quality	Structure	Heuristic
$A \leftarrow A$ $A \overset{\ell}{\leftarrow} A$	$X \leftarrow T$ $S \leftarrow R$	$X \leftarrow Q$ $A \leftarrow C$	$A \leftarrow P \leftarrow S$ $L \leftarrow A, P$ $M \leftarrow A$ $Q \leftarrow A$	$G \leftarrow U$ $S \leftarrow H$ $Q, T \rightarrow C, W, P$
A article ℓ link	X object T post S solution R review	Q question C correction	P problem L collection M classific.	G group U user W request H heuristic

A paragogical decomposition of PlanetMath's activities: "production rules" in the grammar of mathematical behavior

peeragogy project. I started by clustering our PATTERN LANGUAGE DIAGRAM into 5 segments, like this:

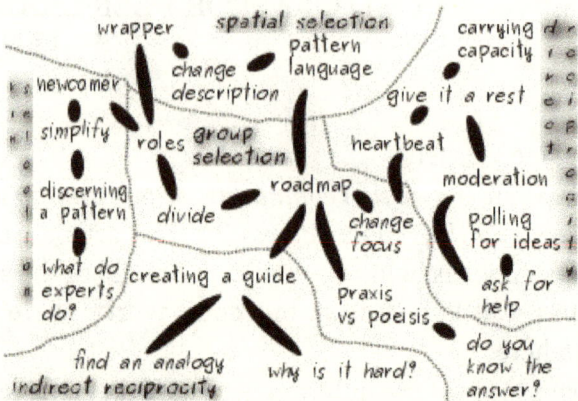

The "key" that shows how things fit together is as follows:

- **Context** ~ Changing context as a decentered center. ~ **Kin selection**

- **Engagement** ~ Meta-learning as a font of knowledge. ~ **Direct reciprocity**

- **Quality** ~ Peers provide feedback that wouldn't be there otherwise. ~ **Indirect reciprocity**

- **Structure** ~ Learning is distributed and nonlinear. ~ **Spatial selection**

- **Heuristic** ~ Realize the dream if you can, then wake up! ~ **Group selection**

The analogies are not perfect, and are meant to help inspire, rather than to constrain, thoughts on the learning/platform design. It's important to remember that Nowak's formalism is meant to be general enough to describe all different kinds of collaboration –

> In a "kin selection" regime, we are working in a "generational" modality; we are looking at what is "related", and this helps to define that which is "unrelated" – the other.

Platform design 175

On PlanetMath, the most important senses of "relatedness" apply to elements of the subject domain. Topics that are linked to one another in the encyclopedia are related. These links can either be implicit term references (which are spotted by PlanetMath's autolinker), or more explicit connections added by authors, readers, or editors. Such links can build an implicit context for a "newcomer" who approaches a given topic.

> *In a "direct reciprocity" regime, we "learning about ourselves" in practice, usually in a social context.*

One of the key legacy features of PlanetMath is that every object in the system is "discussable". You can ask a question about an encyclopedia article, for example, and this will go into a common pool of questions. One of the driving ideas behind the site's (re)design is that every question should help us improve the site, for example, by pointing out a place where the original expository article could be improved. Of course, at the most basic level, we hope that the questions receive good one-off answers (providing a benefit to the initial question-asker). Even the most simple question is a "constructively critical" question. On the level of site semantics, it would be good to keep track of which questions have been answered, and which have not. Questions can be "mutated" into corrections, requests, or mathematical problems to solve.

> *In an "indirect reciprocity" regime, we are building something that may be useful later on.*

Another important legacy feature of PlanetMath is that, unlike Wikipedia, articles are not generally open to the public to edit (though some are). Rather, the typical process of "crowdsourcing" takes place through a corrections mechanism. From an analytical perspective, we might expect corrections to be one of the key ways in which site authors learn from one another. In a sense, the opportunity to get corrections or suggestions pointed out later might be one of the biggest incentives for writing an article in the first place! Offering a correction to someone else is, of course, a

Platform design 176

way to point out one's own knowledgability (as such, a sort of flipside of asking questions). Certain behaviors can help one develop a good reputation (though PlanetMath does not model this very explicitly)... and perhaps even more importantly, a high-quality resource "emerges" from such one-to-one interactions.

> In a "spatial selection" regime, we are again defining an "inside" and "outside", and looking for ways in which the structures that we have identified can fit together.

One of the features that the legacy version of PlanetMath lacked was any sort of support for "problem solving behavior" – which, in mathematics, is actually a pretty essential thing. Rather, the site was set up as a "reference" tool for people who solved problems elsewhere. By moving support for problems, solutions, and reviews onto the PlanetMath site itself, we expect not only to open the "marketplace" up to new kinds of learners (i.e. people working at a more basic level than encylopedia authoring OR people working at a fairly advanced level who are more interested in applications than in theory), but also to get significant improvements to the core knowledge resource itself (the encyclopedia). This is because "an article without an attached problem" is not a very practical article from a learning or application standpoint. Similarly, "a problem without a solution" is lacking something, as is "a solution without a review". Building support for this, and support for people to structure/stage problems with problem sets should help make the site a much more practically useful learning tool.

> In a "group selection" regime, we are building "sets" of activities and patterns (milestones, roles) which can then act as "selectors" for behavior. (This is why I've combined it with the catch-all "heuristic" category.)

Another historical weak point of the legacy site was support for "teams." Thus, for example, one effort to improve PlanetMath's coverage of topics in Real Analysis foundered - because there was no way to gather a critical mass to this project. There are social, technical, and knowledge aspects to this problem. Co-working requires people to be able to join groups, and it requires the groups to be able to structure their workflow. In some sense this is similar to an individual's work being structured by the use of heuristics. A person's choice to apply this strategy instead of that one, or to join this group instead of that one, is in the end a somewhat similar choice.

These notes have shown how the paragogical principles, supplimented with very general theories of collaboration, and some practical observations as examined in the Peeragogy Handbook, can help design a space for learning, which is itself a "learning space" in the sense of knowledge building. Although the case study has focused on mathematics learning, similar reflections would apply to designing other sorts of learning spaces (e.g. to the continued development of the Peeragogy project itself!).

> **Doug Breitbart**: It occurred to me that you could add a learning dimension to the site that sets up the history of math as a series of problems, proofs and theorems that, although already solved, could be re-cast as if not yet solved, and framed as current challenges which visitors could take on (clearly with links to the actual solutions, and deconstruction of how they were arrived at, when the visitor decides to throw in the towel).

Part VIII

Assessment

CHAPTER 22

INTRODUCTION TO PEERAGOGICAL ASSESSMENT

Authors: JOE CORNELI and DAVID PRESTON

This article will be about both assessment in peer learning and an exercise in assessment, as we will try to put our strategy for assessment into practice by evaluating the PEERAGOGY HANDBOOK itself.

Thinking about "contribution"

It is intuitive to say: "learning is adaptation." What else would it be?

Further, since adaptation happens not just on the individual level, but also on the socio-cultural level – anthropologists use the phrase "adaptive strategy" as a synonym for "culture" – we can say that contributions to social adaptation are "paragogical."

Adapting strategies for learning assessment to the peer-learning context

In "EFFECTIVE GRADING: A TOOL FOR LEARNING AND ASSESSMENT," Barbara E. Walvoord and Virginia Johnson Anderson have outlined an approach to grading. They address three questions:

1. Who needs to know, and why?

2. Which data are collected?

3. How does the assessment body analyze data and present findings?

The authors suggest that institutions, departments, and assessment committees should begin with these simple questions and work from them towards anything more complex. These simple questions provide a way to understand - and assess - any strategy for assessment! For example, consider "formative assessment:

> "...which involves constantly monitoring student understanding through a combination of formal and informal measures. Teachers ask searching questions, listen over the shoulders of students working together on a problem, help students assess their own work, and carefully uncover students' thinking [and] react to what they learn by adjusting their teaching, thereby leading students to greater understanding." (Quote from the website for the book "New Frontiers in Formative Assessment".)

In this context, our answers to the questions above would be:

1. Teachers need to know about the way students are thinking about their work, so they can deliver better teaching.

2. Teachers gather lots of details on learning activities by "listening over the shoulders" of students.

3. Teachers apply (hopefully well-informed) analysis techniques that come from their training or experience – and they do not necessarily present their assessments to students directly, but rather, feed it back in the form of improved teaching.

This is very much a "teacher knows best" model! In order to do something like formative assessment among peers, we would have to make quite a few adjustments.

1. At least some of the project participants would have to know how participants are thinking about their work. We might not be able to "deliver better teaching," but perhaps

we could work together to problem-solve when difficulties arise.

2. It may be most convenient for each participant to take on a share of the work, e.g. by maintaining a "learning journal" (which could be shared with other participants). This imposes a certain overhead, but as we remarked elsewhere, "meta-learning is a font of knowledge"! Outside of self-reflection, details about others' learning can sometimes be abstracted from their contributions to the project ("learning analytics" is a whole topic unto itself).

3. If a participant in a "learning project" is bored, frustrated, feeling closed-minded, or for whatever other reason "not learning", then there is definitely a question. But for whom? For the person who isn't learning? For the collective as a whole? We may not have to ponder this conundrum for long: if we go back to the idea that "learning is adaptation", someone who is not learning in a given context will likely leave, and find another context where they can learn more.

This is but one example of an assessment strategy: in addition to "formative assessment", "diagnostic" and "summative" strategies are also quite popular in mainstream education. The main purpose of this section has been to show that when the familiar roles from formal education devolve "to the people", the way assessment looks can change a lot. In the following section, we offer and begin to implement an assessment strategy for evaluating the peeragogy project as a whole.

Case study in peeragogical evaluation: the Peeragogy project itself

We can evaluate this project partly in terms of its main "deliverable," the Peeragogy Handbook (which you are now reading). In particular, we can ask: Is this handbook useful for its intended audience? The "intended audience" could potentially include anyone who is participating in a peer learning project, or who is thinking about starting one. We can also evaluate the learning experience that the co-creators of this handbook have had. Has working on this book been a useful experience for those involved? These are two very different questions, with two different targets for analysis – though the book's co-creators are also part of the "intended audience". Indeed, we might start by asking "has working on this book been useful for us?"

For me (Joe) personally, it has been useful:

to see some more abstract, conceptual, and theoretical ideas (paragogy.net) extended into practical advice (which I'm sure I can personally use), with references to literature I would not have come up with in library or internet searches, and with a bunch of ideas and insights that I wouldn't have come up with on my own. I definitely intend to use this handbook further in my work.

It's true; I do see myself as one of the more involved participants to date, which stands to reason since I'm actually paid to research peer learning, and this project is (in my opinion) one of the most cutting-edge places to talk about that topic! If "you get out of it what you put into it" is true, then, again, as a major contributor, I think I "deserve" a lot. And I'm certainly not the only one: quite a large number of person-hours have been poured into this project by quite a number of volunteers. This should say something!

Nevertheless, one does not need to be a "handbook contributor" at all to get value from the project: if it were otherwise, we might as well just get rid of the book after writing it. Actually, our thought is that this work will indeed have "value" for downstream users, and our choice of legal terms around the book reflects that idea. Anyone downstream is free to use the contents of this book for any purpose whatsoever. For all we know, there will be future users who will add much more to the study and practice of paragogy/peeragogy than any of us have so far. This could happen by putting the ideas to the test, feeding back information on the results to the project (PLEASE DO! - the ultimate assessment of the Peeragogy Handbook will be based on what people actually *do* with it): perhaps further developing the book, developing additional case studies or recipes, and so forth.

In fact, questions about "usefulness" are what we aim to study in our "alpha testing" phase (which is beginning now!).

Conclusion

We can estimate individual learning by examining the real problems solved by the individual. Sometimes those are solved in collaboration with others. If someone only consumes information, they may well be "learning", but there is no way for us to measure that. On the other hand, if they only solve "textbook problems", again, they may be learning and gaining intuition (which is good), but it is still not 100% clear that they are actually learning anything "useful" until they start solving problems that they really care about! So, to assess learning, we do not just measure "contribution" (in terms of quantity of posts or what have you) but instead we measure "contribution to solving real problems". Sometimes that happens very slowly, with lots of practice along the way. Furthermore, at any given point in time, some of the "problems" are actually quite fun and are "solved" by playing! Indeed (as people like Piaget and Vygotsky recognized), if we're interested to know real experts on learning, we should talk with kids, since they learn tons and tons of things.

Recommended reading

- Chris Morgan, Meg O'Reilly, Assessing Open and distance learners (1999), Open University

- Jan Philipp Schmidt, Christine Geith, Stian Håklev, and Joel Thierstein, Peer-To-Peer Recognition of Learning in Open Education

- L.S. Vygotsky: Mind in Society: Development of Higher Psychological Processes

- Reijo Miettinen and Jaakko Virkkunen, Epistemic Objects, Artifacts and Organizational Change, *Organization,* May 2005 ,12: 437-456.

CHAPTER 23

FOLLOWING THE MONEY, ASSESSING PROFITABLITY

Summary

The metrics for learning in corporations are business metrics based on financial data. Managers want to know: "Has the learning experience enhanced the workers' productivity?"

Follow the money

When people ask about the ROI of informal learning, ask them how they measure the ROI of formal learning. Test scores, grades, self-evaluations, attendance, and certifications prove nothing. The ROI of any form of learning is the value of changes in behavior divided by the cost of inducing the change. Like the tree falling over in the forest with no one to hear it, if there's no change in behavior over the long haul, no learning took place. ROI is in the mind of the beholder, in this case, the sponsor of the learning who is going to decide whether or not to continue investing. Because the figure involves judgment, it's never going to be accurate to the first decimal place. Fortunately, it doesn't have to be. Ballpark numbers are solid enough for making decisions.

ASSESSING WORKPLACE LEARNING from JAY CROSS on VIMEO.

The process begins before the investment is made. What degree of change will the sponsor accept as worthy of reinvestment? How are we going to measure that? What's an adequate level of change? What's so low we'll have to adopt a different approach? How much of the change can we attribute to learning? You need to gain agreement on these things beforehand. Monday morning quarterbacking is not credible. It's crazy to assess learning immediately after it occurs. You can see if people are taking part or if they're complaining about getting lost, but you cannot assess what sticks until the forgetting curve has ravaged the learners' memories for a few months. Without reinforcement, people forget most of what they learn in short order. It's beguiling to try to correlate the impact of learning with existing financial metrics like increased revenues or better customer service scores. Done on its own, this approach rarely works because learning is but one of many factors that influence results. Was today's success due to learning or the ad campaign or weak competition or the sales contest or something else? The way to assess how people learn is to ask them. How did you figure out how to do this? Who did you learn this from? How did that change your behavior? How can we make it better? Too time consuming? Not if you interview a representative sample. For example, interviewing less than 100 people out of 2000 yields an answer within 10% nineteen times out of twenty, a higher confidence level than most estimates in business. Interviewing 150 people will give you the right estimate 99% of the time.

CHAPTER 24

RESEARCHING PEERAGOGY

If you have a research bent, by this point, you may be asking yourself questions like these: *How can we understand peer learning better? How can we do research "the peragogical way"? How do we combine research and peer learning?* You may also be asking more technical methodological and instrumentation-level questions: *Do we have a good way to measure learning? Which activities and interventions have the biggest payoff?* This chapter summarizes socio-technical research I did on PlanetMath, using the pattern catalog, as part of my work for my PhD. In the course of the study, I developed 3 new patterns. The first point to make is that although this research was informal, it is nevertheless (at least in my view) highly rigorous. This is because the pattern catalog is a relatively stable, socially agreed upon objct, though it is not fixed for all time. We can use it to help identify "known" patterns, but we can also extend it, as needed, with new patterns - assuming that we can make an argument to explain why the new patterns are needed. The notion of pattern-finding as a process related to, but distinct from abstraction is described by Richard Gabriel, who emphasizes that the "patterns and the social process for applying them are designed to produce organic order through piecemeal growth" [1], p. 31. We can use the rigorous-but-informal notion of an expanding pattern catalog to help address the high-level questions about peeragogical research mentioned above. The three new patterns I present here are: Frontend and Backend, Spanning Set, and Minimum Viable Project. These patterns are both an "outcome" of research in a real peer learning context - and also a reflection on peeragogical research methods. Like the other peeragogy patterns, they are tools you can use in your own work. In particular, I hope this short essay will help you use the peeragogy pattern catalog to constructively evaluate your own peeragogy projects.

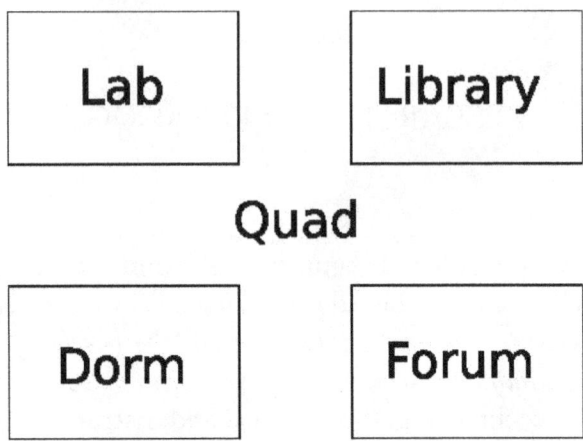

Map of a virtual campus

Study design

The study was based on interviews with users of a new software system that we deployed on PlanetMath.org. In the interviews, we covered a wide range issues, ranging from basic issues of usability all the way to "deep" issues about how people think about mathematics. In this project, I was interested not only in how people collaborate to solve mathematical problems, but how they think about "system level" issues. The design I had in mind is depicted in the figures below. The key idea is that patterns emerge as "paths in the grass", or "desire lines". The idea that learning design has emergent features is not itself new (see e.g. [2]): what's new here is a characterization of the key patterns for *doing* emergent design in a peer learning context.

Initial thematic analysis

Before describing the new patterns, I will briefly summarize the themes I identified in the interviews. This can serve as an overview of the current features and shortcomings of PlanetMath system for people who are not familiar with it.

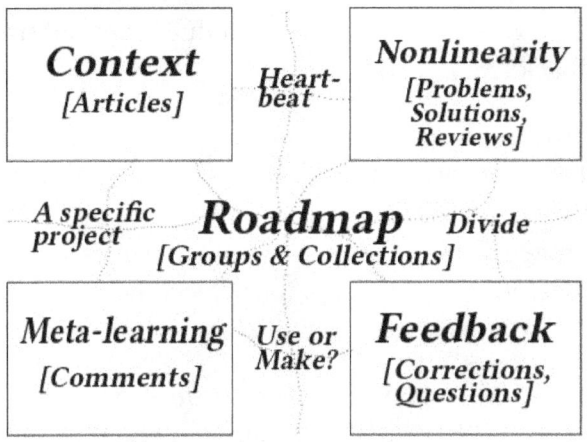

Peeragogy patterns as loci for "paths in the grass"

- **"Necessary but not sufficient".** Users identified a range of essential features, like a critical mass of other users to talk to.

- **"Nice to have".** It was also easy to identify a bunch of cool new "dream" features.

- **Challenges with writing mathematics.** PlanetMath uses LaTeX, which isn't entirely easy to learn (however, we could adapt the software to help new users get started).

- **Progressive problem solving.** The new PlanetMath contains problems and solutions, but no easy way to talk about conjectures. Users would like a better way to share and discuss work-in-progress.

- **Personal history, social constructivism.** Better features for tracking and, where appropriate, sharing, personal history would help users make sense of what's happening in the site.

- **Regulating learning in a social/mediated context.** Different users would look for different things to keep them on track (e.g. expert guidance, or a due "sense of urgency" in feedback from peers).

- **Comparison with roles in other contexts.** Many users expect a "service delivery" style that is not entirely consistent with the "open" production model used in a free/open, volunteer-driven project. We need to work more on responsiveness in every aspect of the project (keeping in mind that most participants are volunteers).

- **Concreteness as a criterion of quality.** "Knowing what you can do," both with the software and with the content, is important. On the content level, pictures help.

- **Personalization and localization.** The system has a practically unlimited potential for personalization, although many basic personalized interaction modes have not been built yet.

Pattern analysis

At the next level of analysis, the themes extracted above were further analysed in relationship to the peeragogy pattern catalog.

Frontend and Backend

Although mathematics is a relatively formal domain, many of the motivations for using PlanetMath map onto what Zimmerman and Campillo call informal problem solving [3]. Informal problems are are personally defined and possess openended boundary conditions, i.e., are situated within an "open world." "Formal" motivations are are more likely to be addressed by some variant of a "look-up" approach - for instance, many such problems can be solved by reading the manual. They do not require the complex, discursive, process of peer supported problem solving. Acquaintance with the more basic formal features of mathematical problem solving are typically seen to be a prerequisite for the more informal activities of mathematics research. This points to the continued importance of a coherent body of mathematical knowledge in the form of a well-structured reference resource. This dichotomy suggest a new and important pattern. This pattern could be called Frontend and Backend. The "frontend" of a system is typically associated with the formal structural features, while the backend is often associated with "informal features." The Frontend and Backend pattern is related to the pattern of the "Newcomer" pattern, since typically one will not expect the user of a system to know how to, or to be motivated to, work with backend features of a system until they have mastered at least some of the frontend features. It would be rare to find an auto mechanic who did not know how to drive. David Cavallo wrote about an "engine culture" in rural Thailand, in which structurally open systems made some of the "backend" features of internal combustion engines a part of daily life [4]. In PlanetMath, we have an "open engine", but not necessarily an open engine culture (users expect a level of service provision). The Frontend and Backend pattern clearly lends itself to standard service provision, but it can also be part of paragogical activity. For example, sophisticated and committed users of the PlanetMath website could focus energy on supporting individual newcomers, by helping them develop a high-quality sub-site on their topic of interest ([RSP8], [RSP10]). Such effort would simultaneously inform the development of backend features, and help raise the profile of the site as a whole. The pattern is in this way associated with A Specific Project and with the Divide pattern.

Spanning Set

You may be able to get what you need without digging - but if you do need to dig, it would be very good to get some indication about which direction to dig in. At the content level, this might be achieved by using high-level "topic articles" as a map to the content. But there is another broader interpretation of this pattern that related to but distinct from Frontend and Backend - we call this the Spanning Set. In general, the Spanning Set might be made up of people, or media objects. In a standard course model, there is one central node, the teacher, who is responsible for all teaching and course communication. In large online courses, this model can be is scaled up:

> **Anonymous study participant**: [E]veryone's allocated a course tutor, who might take on just a half-dozen students - so, they're not the overall person in charge of the course, by any means.

Another version is the classical master/apprentice system, in which every apprentice is supervised by a certified master. In the typical online Q&A context, these roles are made distributed, and are better modeled by power laws than by formal gradations. A "spanning set" of peer tutors could help shift the exponent attached to the power law in massive courses. We can imagine a given discussion group of 100 persons that is divided according to the so-called 90/9/1 RULE, so that 90 lurk, 9 contribute a little, and 1 creates the content. This is what one might observe, for example, in a classroom with a lecture format. We could potentially shift the system by breaking the group up, so that each of the 9 contributors leads a small group of 10 persons, at which point, chances are good that some of the former lurkers would be converted into contributors. At a more semantic level, we can advance the five paragogical principles and their various analogues as a candidate description of the fundamental categories and relationships relevant to peer learning. In practice, principles can only provide the most visible "frontend", and an actual spanning set is comprised of emergent patterns. In PlanetMath, this would arise from combining several different features, like a "start menu" that shows what can be done with the site, a Heartbeat built of recurring meetings, and topic-level guides to content. (Note: as a project with an encyclopedic component, PlanetMath itself can be used to span and organize a significantly larger body of existing material.)

Minimum Viable Project

The Minimum Viable Product approach to software development is about putting something out there to see if the customer bites [5]. Another approach, related to the pattern we just discussed, is to make it clear what people can do with what's there and see if they engage. We might call this the Minimum Viable Project, an adjunct to the "Roadmap" pattern, and a new interpretation of the earlier pattern A Specific Project. One way to strengthen the PlanetMath project as a whole would be to focus on support for individual projects. The front page of the website could be redesigned so that the top-level view of the site is project focused. Thus, instead of collecting all of the posts from across the site - or even all of the threads from across the site - the front page could collect succinct summary information on recently active projects, and list the number of active posts in each, after the model of Slashdot stories or StackExchange questions. For instance, each Mathematics Subject Classification could be designated as a "sub-project", but there could be many other cross-cutting or smaller-scale projects.

Frontend and Backend (*pragma*)
Principles and features

Minimum Viable Project (*praxis*)
A Specific Project, Roadmap, Heartbeat, Divide, Use or Make

Spanning Set (*pratto*)
Paths in the grass

Paragogical emergent design: a tool for conviviality

Summary

This chapter has used the approach suggested by Figure 2 to expand the peeragogy pattern language. It shows that the peeragogy pattern language provides a "meta-model" that can be used to develop emergent order relative to given boundary conditions. As new structure forms, this becomes part of the boundary conditions for future iterations. This method is a suitable form for a theory of peer learning and peer production in project-based and cross-project collaborations - a tool for conviviality in the sense of Ivan Illich. Although this model is informal, it does suggest one direction for answering the technical questions posed at the outset of the chapter: in peeragogy, we can measure learning as a feature of the growth and refinement of the pattern catalog.

References

1. Gabriel, R. (1996). Patterns of Software. Oxford University Press New York.

2. Luckin, R. (2010). Re-designing learning contexts: technology-rich, learner-centred ecologies. Routledge.

3. Zimmerman, B. J. & Campillo, M. (2003). Motivating self-regulated problem solvers. In J. Davidson & R. Sternberg (Eds.), The psychology of problem solving (pp. 233-262). Cambridge University Press New York, NY.

4. Cavallo, D. P. (2000). Technological Fluency and the Art of Motorcycle Maintenance: Emergent design of learning environments (Doctoral dissertation, Massachusetts Institute of Technology).

5. Ries, E. (2011). The Lean Startup: How today's entrepreneurs use continuous innovation to create radically successful businesses. Crown Pub.

Part IX

Technologies, Services, and Platforms

CHAPTER 25

INTRODUCTION TO TECHNOLOGIES FOR PEERAGOGY

It is tempting to bring a list of technologies out as a glorious cookbook. We need a 1/2 cup of group writing tools, 2 tsp. of social network elements, a thick slice of social bookmarking, and some sugar, then put it in the oven for 1 hour for 350 degrees.

We have created a broad features/functions list for Handbook readers to reflect upon and consider. The joy of this list is that you can consider alternatives for the way you communicate and work while you are planning the project, or can add in new elements to solve communications gaps or create new tools.

However, too many tools spoil the broth. In the writing of this Handbook, we found that out firsthand. We spent a lot of marvelous energy exploring different tools to collaborate, curate information, do research, tag resources, and adjudicate among all of our points of view. In looking at groups working with the various MOOCs, as another example, different groups of students often camp in different social media technologies to work. In large courses, students often have to be pushed into various social media tools to "co-create" with great protest and lots of inertia. And finally, co-learning groups often come from very different backgrounds, ages, and stages of life, with very different tools embedded in their current lives. Do we have time for three more tools in our busy days? Do more tools help or interfere in our work?

In this section, we'll share with you a few issues:

- What technologies are most useful in peer learning? What do we use them for? What features or functions help our co-learning process?

- How do we decide (a) as a group and (b) for the group on

what tools we can use? Do we decide upfront, or grow as we go?

- How do we coach and scaffold each other on use of tools?

- How much do the tool choices impact the actual outcome of our learning project?

- What are the different roles that co-learners can take in co-teaching and co-coaching the technology affordances/assumptions in the project to make others' lives easier?

Features and Considerations

We will begin below with a discussions of "features" and initial considerations, and then move to a broader "Choose Your Own Adventure"-style matrix of features leading to a wide variety of collaboration-based technology tools online.

Technologies and Features

As we will share in the extensive list below, there are abundant tools now available – both for free and for pay – to bring great features to our co-learning endeavors. It is tempting to grab a group of fancy tools and bring the group into a fairly complex tool environment to find the perfect combination of resources. The challenge: as Adult Learners, we seek both comfort and context in our lives (Schein, 1997, 2004). In choosing tools as Brands and technologies, we can ignore the features themselves and what we need as parts of the puzzle for learning. We also can have anxiety about our self-beliefs around computers and technology, which in turn can limit our abilities (COMPEAU & HIGGINS, 1995).

Before we get to Brands and choices, it helps to ask a few questions about the learning goals and environments:

- What do we need as features, and at what stage of the learning process?

- What are we already comfortable with, individually and as a group?

- Do we want to stay with comfortable existing tools, or do we want to stretch, or both?

- What types of learners do we have in this group? Technologically advanced? Comfortable with basics?

- Do we want to invest the time to bring the whole group up to speed on tools? Do all the group members agree on this? Do we want to risk alienating members by making them invest time in new resources?

- We know that our use will migrate and adapt. Do we want to plan for adaptation? Observe it? Learn from it? Make that change intentional as we go?

Researchers over the years have heavily examined these questions of human, technology, and task fit in many arenas. HUMAN-COMPUTER INTERACTION researchers have looked at "fit" and "adaptive behavior," as well as how the tools can affect how the problem is presented in the work (TE'ENI, 2006). Creativity support tools (SHNEIDERMAN, 2002) have a whole line of design research, as has the field of COMPUTER-SUPPORTED COLLABORATIVE WORK SYSTEMS (CSCW). For co-learners and designers interested in the abundance in this space, we've added some additional links below.

We here will make this a bit easier. For your co-learning environment, you may want to do one or two exercises in your decision planning:

- What **features do you need**? Do you need collaboration? Graphic models? Places to work at the same time (synchronous)? Between meetings (asynchroous)?

- What are the group members **already using** as their personal learning platforms? It also makes sense to do an inventory about what the group already has as their learning platforms. I'm doing that with another learning group right now. People are much more comfortable – as we also have found in our co-creation of this Handbook – creating and co-learning in tools with which they already are comfortable. Members can be co-teachers to each other – as we have have – in new platforms.

- What **type of tools**, based on the features that we need, shall we start out with? RESNICK AT AL. (2005)looked at technology tools having

  – Low thresholds (easy to get people started)

  – Wide walls (able to bring in lots of different situations and uses) and

  – High ceilings (able to do complex tasks as the users and uses adapt and grow).

What are important features needed for co-creation and **working together**? In other pages above, we talk abundantly about roles and co-learning challenges. These issues also are not new; DOURISH & BELLOTTII BACK IN 1992 for example, shared long-standing issues in computer-supportive collaborative work online about how we are aware of the information from others, passive vs. active generation of information about collaborators, etc. These challenges used to be "solved" by software designers in individual tools. Now that tools are open, abundant, and diverse, groups embrace these same challenges when choosing between online resources for co-learning.

Which of these will be important to your group work? Keep in mind – your needs for tools, plus how the group uses them, will change as the co-learning project moves along. Are you willing to change tools during the project as your needs and users change, or do you want to plan on tools that are great in all these dimensions at the start?

Useful Uses and fancy Features of Technological Tools

From here, we will help you think about what might be possible, linking to features and solution ideas.

We start with ways to ask the key questions: What do you want to do and why? We will start with features organized around several different axes:

- TIME/PLACE
- STAGES OF ACTIVITIES AND TASKS
- SKILL BUILDING/BLOOM'S TAXONOMY
- USE CASES, and
- LEARNING FUNCTIONS.

Each will link to pages that will prompt you with features, functionality, and technology tool ideas.

Time/Place

We can further break down tools into whether they create or distribute, or whether we can work simultaneously (synchronous) or at our own times (ascynchronous). To make elements of time and place more visual, BAECKER (1995) created a CSCW Matrix, bringing together time and place functions and needs:

Some tools are synchronous, such as Google+ Hangouts, Blackboard Collaborate, and Adobe Connect, while others let us work asynchronously, such as wikis, forums, and Google Docs. We seem to be considering here mostly tools good for group work, but not for solo, while many others are much easier solo or in smaller groups.

Stages of Activities and Tasks

DAN SHNEIDERMAN (2002) has simplified the abundant models in this area (e.g., Couger and Cave) with a clear model of 4 general activities and 8 tasks in creation for individuals, which we can lean on as another framework for co-creation in co-learning.

Activities

Tasks

Collect

- Searching
- Visualizing

Relate

- Consulting Others

Create

- Thinking (Free Association)
- Exploring
- Composing
- Reviewing

Distribute

- Disseminating

Tools and functions won't be clear cut between areas. For example, some tools are more focused on being generative, or for creating content. Wikis, Etherpad, Google docs, and others usually have a commenting/talk page element, yet generating content is the primary goal and discursive/consultative functions are in service of that. Some tools are discursive, or focused on working together for the creative element of "relating" above – Blackboard Collaborate, the social media class room forums, etc.

Skill Building (Cognitive, a la Bloom's Taxonomy, see below)

Given that we are exploring learning, we can look to Bloom's Taxonomy (revised, ANDERSON & KRATHWOHL, 2001) for guidance as to how we can look at knowledge support. Starting at the bottom, we have:

- Remembering, as a base;

- Understanding,

- Applying,

- Analyzing,

- Evaluating, and then, at the top,

- Creating.

We could put "search" in the Remembering category above. Others [need to re-find and cite] contest that Search, done well, embraces most of the Bloom's elements above. Samantha Penney has created a Bloom´s Digital Taxonomy Pyramid of tools for learning (cc 3.0 – HTTP://WWW.USI.EDU/DISTANCE/BDT.HTM).

Use Cases (I want to....)

Technologies can be outlined according to the need they serve or use case they fulfill. Examples: If we need to 'curate', Pearl Trees is an option. To 'publish' or 'create', we can look to a wiki or wordpress. Other choices might be great in order to 'collaborate', etc.

One challenge is that tools are not that simple. As we look more closely at the technologies today, we need to reach more broadly to add multiple tags to them. For example Twitter can be used for "Convening a group," for "micro-blogging," for "research," etc.

- Collaborate with a Group

- Create Community

- Curate Information (select content, contextualize, and share it)

- Research

- Publish Information

- Create Learning Activities

- Make Something

These plans get more complex, as you are making a group of decisions about tool functionality in order to choose what combination works for use cases. It may be most useful to use a concept map (a tech tool) to think about the needs and combinations that you would bring together to achieve each Use Case or Learning Module.

Technology Features/Functions

We have not made this easy! There are lots of moving elements and options here, none of them right for everything, and some of them fabulous for specific functions and needs. Some have the low thresholds but may not be broad in scope. Some are broad for many uses; others are specific task-oriented tools. That is some of the charm and frustration.

Weaving all of the above together, we have brought together a shared taxonomy for us to discuss and think about co-learning technology features and functions, which we present as an appendix below. This connects various technology features within an expanded version of Ben Shneiderman's creativity support tools framework. We've created this linked toolset with multiple tags, hopefully making it easier for you to evaluate which tool suits best the necessities of the group. Please consider this a starting point for your own connected exploration.

Appendix: Features and Functions

Weaving all of these frameworks together, we have brought together a shared taxonomy for us to discuss and think about co-learning technology features and functions. We have connected various technology features with an expanded version of Ben Shneiderman's creativity support tools framework. For convenience, and to help keep it up to date, we're publishing this resource ON GOOGLE DOCS (HTTP://GOO.GL/H02FMA).

References

- Anderson, L. W., & Krathwohl, D. R. (Eds.). (2001). *A taxonomy for learning, teaching and assessing: A revision of Bloom's Taxonomy of educational objectives: Complete edition.* New York, NY: Longman.

- Baecker, R., GRUDIN, J., BUXTON, W., & GREENBERG, & (eds.) (1995): *Readings in Human-Computer Interaction: Toward the Year 2000.* New York, NY: Morgan Kaufmann Publishers

- Compeau, D.R., & Higgins, C.A. (1995, June). Computer Self-Efficacy: Development of a Measure and Initial Test. *MIS Quarterly, 19*, (2), 189-211.

- Dourish, P. & Bellotti, V. (1992). Awareness and coordination in shared workspaces. In *Proceedings of the 1992 ACM conference on Computer-supported cooperative work* (CSCW '92). ACM, New York, NY, USA, 107-114. DOI=10.1145/143457.143468 http://doi.acm.org/10.1145/143457.143468

- Resnick, M, Myers, B, Nakakoji, K, Shneiderman, B, Pausch, R, Selker, T. & Eisenberg, M (2005). Design principles for tools to support creative thinking. *Institute for Software Research*. Paper 816. http://repository.cmu.edu/isr/816

- Schein, E. H. (1997). *Organizational learning as cognitive re-definition: Coercive persuasion revisited*. Cambridge, MA: Society for Organizational Learning.

- Schein, E. H. (2004). *Organizational culture and leadership*. San Francisco, CA: Jossey-Bass.

- Shneiderman, B. (2002). Creativity support tools. *Commun. ACM* 45, 10 (October 2002), 116-120. DOI=10.1145/570907.570945 http://doi.acm.org/10.1145/570907.570945

- Te'eni, D. (2006). Designs that fit: An overview of fit conceptualizations in HCI. In *Human-Computer Interaction and Management Information Systems: Foundations*, edited by P. Zhang and D. Galletta, pp. 205-221, Armonk, NY: M.E. Sharpe.

Additional Research for Interested Co-Learners

- Irene Greif and Sunil Sarin (1987): Data Sharing in Group Work, ACM Transactions on Office Information Systems, vol. 5, no. 2, April 1987, pp. 187-211.

- Irene Greif (ed.) (1988): Computer-Supported Cooperative Work: A Book of Readings, San Mateo, CA: Morgan Kaufman.

- Irene Greif (1988): Remarks in panel discussion on "CSCW: What does it mean?", CSCW '88. Proceedings of the Conference on Computer-Supported Cooperative Work, September 26-28, 1988, Portland, Oregon, ACM, New York, NY.

- Kamnersgaard, 1988

- Vessey & Galletta, 1991

- Norman, 2001, 2003

- DeSanctis & Pool, 2004

	Same Time (Synchronous)	Different Time (Ascynronous)
Same Place (Colocated)	**Face-to-Face:** Display-focused (e.g., Smartboards)	**Continuous Task:** Groupware, project management
Different Place (Remote)	**Remote Interaction:** Videoconference, IM, Chat, Virtual Worlds	**Communication & Coordination:** Email, bulletin boards, Wikis, blog, workflow tools

CHAPTER 26

FORUMS

Author: Howard Rheingold

Forums are web-based communication media that enable groups of people to conduct organized multimedia discussions about multiple topics over a period of time. Selecting the right kind of platform for forum conversations is important, as is know-how about facilitating ongoing conversations online. Forums can be a powerful co-learning tool for people who may have never met face-to-face and could be located in different time zones, but who share an interest in co-learning. Asynchronous media such as forums (or simple email distribution lists or GOOGLE DOCS) can be an important part of a co-learning toolkit that also includes synchronous media from face-to-face meetups to GOOGLE+ HANGOUTS or webinars via BLACKBOARD COLLABORATE, ADOBE CONNECT, or the open source webconferencing tool, BIG BLUE BUTTON (discussed a little later in the handbook).

What is a forum and why should a group use it?

A forum, also known as a message board, BBS, threaded discussion, or conferencing system, affords asynchronous, many-to-many, multimedia discussions for large groups of people over a period of time. That means that people can read and write their parts of the discussion on their own schedule, that everyone in a group can communicate with everyone else, and that graphics, sounds, and videos can accompany text. The best forums index discussion threads by topic, title, tag, date, and/or author and also keep track of which threads and entries (also known as posts) each logged-in participant has already read, making it possible to click on a "show me all the new posts and threads" link each time a participant logs in. This particular form of conversational medium meets the need for organizing conversations after they reach a certain level of complexity. For example, if twenty people want to discuss five subjects over ten days, and each person makes one comment on each subject every day, that makes for one thousand messages in each participant's mailbox. On email lists, when the conversation drifts from the original topic, the subject line usually does not change, so it makes it difficult to find particular discussions later.

Forums make possible a new kind of group discussion that unfolds over days, weeks, and months, in a variety of media. While blogs are primarily about individual voice, forms can be seen as the voice of a group. The best forum threads are not serial collections of individual essays, but constitute a kind of discourse where the discussion becomes more than the sum of its individual posts. Each participant takes into account what others have said, builds on previous posts, poses and answers questions of others, summarize, distill, and concludes.

THIS SHORT VIDEO ADDRESSES WHY TO USE FORUMS. **(Reload this page if you don't see the player)**

This short piece on GUIDELINES FOR DISCUSSION BOARD WRITINGis useful, as is this short piece on SHAPING A CULTURE OF CONVERSATION. Lively forums with substantial conversation can glue together the disparate parts of a peeragogy group – the sometimes geographically dispersed participants, texts, synchronous chats, blogs, wikis and other co-learning tools and elements. Forum conversations are an art in themselves and forums for learning communities are a specific genre. Reading the resources linked here – and communicating about them – can help any peeragogy group get its forums off to a good start

How to start fruitful forum discussions:

In most contexts, starting a forum with a topic thread for introductions tends to foster the sense of community needed for

Forums

valuable conversations. THIS SHORT PIECE ON HOW TO HOST GOOD CONVERSATIONS ONLINE offers general advice. In addition to introductions, it is often helpful to start a topic thread about which new topic threads to create – when everybody has the power to start a new thread and not everybody knows how forums work, a confusing duplication of conversations can result, so it can be most useful to make the selection of new topic threads a group exercise. A topic thread to ask questions about how to use the forum can prevent a proliferation of duplicate questions. It helps to begin a forum with a few topic threads that invite participation in the context of the group's shared interest "Who is your favorite photographer" for a group of photographers, for example, or "evolution of human intelligence" for a group interested in evolution and/or human intelligence. Ask questions, invite candidate responses to a challenge, make a provocative statement and ask for reactions.

Whether or not you use a rubric for assessing individual participants' forum posts, this guide to HOW FORUM POSTS ARE EVALUATED by one professor can help convey the difference between a good and a poor forum conversation.:

4 Points - The posting(s) integrates multiple viewpoints and weaves both class readings and other participants' postings into their discussion of the subject.

3 Points - The posting(s) builds upon the ideas of another participant or two, and digs deeper into the question(s) posed by the instructor.

2 Points - A single posting that does not interact with or incorporate the ideas of other participants' comments.

1 Point - A simple "me too" comment that neither expands the conversation nor demonstrates any degree of reflection by the student.

0 Points - No comment.

Selecting a forum platform

- You don't want a forum for discussions among two or three people; you do want a forum for discussions among half a dozen or five thousand people.

- You don't want a forum for exchanges of short duration (an hour, a day or two) among any number of people; you do want a forum for ongoing conversations that can continue for months.

- You don't want a forum if blogs with comment threads will do – blogs with comments afford group discourse, but is not easily indexed and discourse gets complicated with more than a dozen or so bloggers and commenters.

If you do want to select a platform for forum discourse, you will want to decide whether you have the technical expertise available to install the software on your own server or whether you want to look for a hosted solution. Cost is an issue.

Fortunately, an online forum maven by the name of DAVID WOOLEY has been keeping an up-to-date list of available software and services for more than a decade:

- FORUM SOFTWARE FOR THE WEB

- FORUM AND MESSAGE BOARD HOSTING SERVICES

These 2003 SUGGESTIONS ON HOW TO CHOOSE A FORUM by Howard Rheingold can be helpful. If blogs with comments afford a kind of networked individualistic discourse, and video conferencing emulates face-to-face meeting, forums can be seen as a channel for expression of the group voice. When people react to and build on each other's comments, they can learn to act as a collective intelligence as well as a collection of individuals who are communicating in order to learn.

Resources:

WHY USE FORUMS? Video by Howard Rheingold. THE ART OF HOSTING GOOD CONVERSATIONS ONLINE. Article by Howard Rheingold. GUIDELINES FOR DISCUSSION BOARD WRITING. Article by Professor Edward J. Gallagher. SHAPING A CULTURE OF CONVERSATION: The Discussion Board and Beyond. Another artcicle by Professor Edward J. Gallagher. IMPROVING THE USE OF DISCUSSION BOARDS. Article on the site of the Worcester Polytechnic Institute, about the evaluation of forum posts by one professor. FORUM SOFTWARE FOR THE WEB. List by David R. Woolley. FORUM & MESSAGE BOARD HOSTING SERVICES. List by David R. Woolley. Tools: GOOGLE DOCS. Video by Nundu JanakiRam. GOOGLE+ HANGOUTS. Introduction on the Google site. BLACKBOARD COLLABORATE. Product description. ADOBE CONNECT. Product description. BIG BLUE BUTTON. Site of the organization.

Relevant articles in Peeragogy Handbook:

CO-FACILITATION TECHNOLOGIES, SERVICES AND PLATFORMS CONNECTIVISM IN PRACTICE, How to Organize a MOOC

CHAPTER 27

WIKI

In the context of P2P-learning, a wiki platform can be a useful and powerful collaboration tool. This section will help you understand what a wiki is and what it is not, why you should use it, how to choose a wiki engine and finally how you could use it in a P2P context. Some examples of P2P-learning projects run on wikis will help you see the potential of the tool.

What is a wiki?

For WARD CUNNINGHAM father of the wiki, "a wiki is a freely expandable collection of interlinked Web 'pages', a hypertext system for storing and modifying information - a database, where each page is easily editable by any user with a forms-capable Web browser client" [1]

According to Wikipedia : "a wiki is a website whose users can add, modify, or delete its content via a web browser using a simplified markup language or a rich-text editor" [2]

You can watch this CommonCraft video WIKI IN PLAIN ENGLISH to better understand what a wiki is.

What differentiates the wiki from other co-editing tools?

The previous definitions show that a wiki is a "website," in other words it is composed of pages that are connected together by hyperlinks.In additiont every authorized person (not all wikis are totally open like Wikipedia) can edit the pages from a web browser, reducing time and space constrains. In case one saves a mistake or for any other reason would like to go back to a previous version, a feature called "history" allows users to see previous versions and to roll back any of them. This version history allows also to compare versions avoiding the cluttered of the "commentaries rainbow" we are used too in popular Word processors. For example if you work on a wiki page, and come back later on, you will be able to catch up by comparing your last version with the lastest version of someone else.

Tools like GOOGLE DOCS or ETHERPAD are design to enable co-editing on a single document. This can be seen as a "wiki way" of working on a document as it is web based and includes versioning. But it is not a wiki because a single document is not a website. Those tools offer realtime collaboration which wikis do not and are so far easier to use for beginners as they work in WYSIWYG mode, which many wikis do not support. However, the advanced features WIKI MARKUP LANGUAGE make it a more powerful tool. In summary, tools like Googles Docs or Etherpad are a great way to quickly collaborate (synchronously, asynchronously, or a mixture of both) on a single document for free, with a low barrier to entry and no technical support. (Note that Etherpad does have a "wiki-links" plugin that can allow it to be used in a more wiki-like way; HACKPAD is another real-time editing tool that prominently features linking – and it claims to be "the best wiki ever".)

Using a real wiki engine is more interesting for bigger projects and allows a huge number of users to collaborate on the same platform. A wiki reduces the coordination complication as e-mails exchanges are no more needed to coordinate a project. On the other hand it can help us deal with complexity [3][4] especially if you put basic simple rules in place like the Wikipedia's NEUTRAL POINT OF VIEW to allow every participant to share her or his ideas.

Going back to the continuum we talked about before, some tools like Moodle, SharePoint, WordPress, Drupal or others have build in wiki features. Those features can be good but will typically not be as good for wiki-building purposes as a well-developed special-purpose wiki engine. In other words, those tools main focus is not the wiki, which is only a secondary feature. When you choose a real wiki engine like MEDIAWIKI, TIKI, FOSWIKI, etc., the wiki will be your platform, not a feature of it. For example if you start a wiki activity in a Moodle course, this wiki will be only visible to a specific group of students and searchable only to those students. On the other hand if your learning platform is a wiki, the whole platform will be searchable to all members regarding their permissions. We are not saying here that a wiki is better than other tools but if you need a wiki engine to address your needs you may consider going with a strong wiki engine rather than a "micro-wiki" engine embedded in an other tool.

Why use a wiki?

Those are the main reasons you should consider a wiki for your peer learning projects :

- to reduce coordination complication by having a central and always up to date place to store your content. You will reduce e-mail usage drasticly, and have access to your content from everywhere using any operating system

- to keep track of the evolution of your project and be able to view or roll back any previous version of a wiki page using the history feature

- to make links between wiki pages to connect ideas and people but also make links to external URL's. This last possibility is very handy to cite your sources

- to deal with complexity. As a wiki allows anyone to contribute, if you set some easy rules like Wikipedia's NPOV (Neutral Point of View), you will be able to catch more complexity as you will allow everyone to express his or her opinion. Wikis also integrate a forum or comment feature that will help you solve editing conflicts

- to deal with work in progress. A wiki is a great tool to capture an on going work

- to support transparency by letting every members of the community see what others are doing

Wiki

- to support a network structure as a wiki is by essence an horizontal tool. Using a hyperlinks you will be able to : "jump by a single clic from a network node to the other, from a computer to an other, from one information to the other, from one univers to the other, from one brain to the other." Translated from [5]

How to choose a wiki engine?

You will find more than a hundred different wiki engines. The first main distinction is between open source ones that are free to download and commercial ones you will have to pay for. You will find powerful engines on both sides open source and commercial. Sometimes the open source ones look less polished at first sight but are backed by a strong community and offer a lot of customization possibilities. The commercial are sold like a package, they are nicely presented but often they offer less customization on the user side and additional feature or custom made tools will cost you an extra fee. The second distinction that we can make is between wiki farms and self-hosted wikis. The WIKI FARM is a hosting service you can find for both open source or commercial wikis. The goal of those farms is to simplify the hosting of individual wikis. If you don't want to choose a wiki farm hosting, you will have to host the wiki on your own server. This will give you more latitude and data privacy but will require more technical skills and cost you maintenance fees.

The WIKIMATRIX web site will help you choose the best wiki for your needs. It allows you to compare the features of more than a hundred wiki engines. HERE is the top ten list of the best wiki engines by Ward Cunningham.

How can a wiki be useful in a peeragogy project?

A wiki is a good tool collaborative projects and a specially suited for work in progress as you can easily track changes using the history, compare those version and if necessary roll back a previous versions. In other words, nothing gets lost.

Here are some ideas about how to use a wiki in a peeragogy project :

- **Use a wiki as your learning platform.** It can also support Massive Open Online Courses (MOOCs). A wiki will help you organize your learning context. You can choose to give access to your wiki only to the project participants or open it to the public like Wikipedia. Using hyperlinking, you will operationalize the theory of connectivism by connecting nodes together. As a learning platform wikis are powerful because you can easily see what others are doing, share with them, get inspired, merge ideas or link to ideas. In other words, it creates emulation between learners. For additional ressources about wiki in education follow this Diigo link.

- **Manage your peeragogy project.** A wiki is an excellent tool for project collaboration. Above all, the wiki can be a central place for peer learners to write or link to content. Even if you use several technologies to run your project as we did to write this handbook, at the end of the day, all the content can be centralized on a wiki using direct writing on wiki pages or hyperlinks. This way members can access the content from anywhere and from any device connected to the internet using any platform or application and they will always see the most recent version while being able to browse through the versions history to understand what has changed since their last visit.

- **Publish your project.** As a wiki is a website you can easily use it to show your work to the world. Regarding web design, don't forget that a wiki can look way better than a Wikipedia page if you customize it

Examples of peeragogy projects run on wikis

Appropedia is a wiki site for collaborative solutions in sustainability, poverty reduction and international develop-

MENT through the use of sound PRINCIPLES and APPROPRIATE TECHNOLOGY and the sharing of wisdom and PROJECT information. The site is open to stakeholders to find, create and improve scalable and adaptable solutions.

TEAHOUSE is a peeragogy project run on a wiki that gives newcomers a place to learn about Wikipedia culture and get feedback from experienced Wikipedians.

What are the best practices when using a wiki?

- **Cofacilitation** – help each other learn, help each other administer

- **Self-election** – enable people to choose what they want to work on, at their own pace, in their own way

- **Communication** – use comment threads and talk pages to discuss wiki changes

- **Documenting changes** – most wikis enable editors to write very brief descriptions of their edits

- **Rules** – keep rules at a minimum level to avoid chaos without constraining creativity

- **Fun** – make it fun for people to contribute

Sources

1. Leuf, Bo, et Ward, Cunningham. 2001. The Wiki way : quick collaboration on the Web. Boston: Addison-Wesley, xxiii, 435 p. p.14

2. WIKI on Wikipedia

3. Andrus, Calvin D. 2005. TOWARD A COMPLEX ADAPTATIVE INTELLIGENCE COMMUNITY - THE WIKI AND THE BLOG. Studies in Intelligence. vol. 49, no 3. Online :

4. Barondeau, Régis. 2010. LA GESTION DE PROJET CROISE LE WIKI. École des Sciences de la Gestion, Université du Québec à Montréal, 180 pp.

5. Ayache, Gérard. 2008. Homo sapiens 2.0 : introduction à une histoire naturelle de l'hyperinformation. Paris: Milo, 284 p. p.179

CHAPTER 28

REAL-TIME MEETINGS

Author: HOWARD RHEINGOLD

Summary

Web services that enable broadband-connected learners to communicate in real time via audio, video, slides, whiteboards, chat, and screen-sharing enable learning groups to add some of the audio-visual dimensions familiar from synchronous face-to-face communication to otherwise asynchronous platforms such as forums, blogs, and wikis. This article includes resources for finding and evaluating appropriate for-free or for-fee platforms, tips on participative activities for real-time meetings, and suggestions for blending real-time and asynchronous media.

Real-time meeting media

This Peeragogy Handbook was conceived and constructed by a group of people on four continents who had not met and had not known about each other before we began meeting online. The process involves asynchronous media, including forums, wikis, social bookmarking groups, and Wordpress, but it probably would never have cohered into a group capable of collective action if it had not been for the real-time meetings where we were able to see each other's faces, hear each other's voices, use a whiteboard as an anonymous agenda-generator, exchange links in chat, show each other examples through screen-sharing. Together, the asynchronous and real-time media enabled us to begin to see ourselves as an effective group. We used both real-time and asynchronous tools to work out processes for creating, refining, and publishing the Handbook, to divide labor, decide on platforms and processes, to collaboratively compose and edit articles, and to design and add graphical and video elements. In particular, we used the BLACKBOARD COLLABORATE platform, a web-service that enables up to 50 people at a time to meet in a multimedia, recordable, meeting room for around $500/year. We've experimented with other paid platforms, such as ADOBE CONNECT (about the same price as Collaborate), and when we meet in groups of ten or less, we often use the free and recordable GOOGLE+ HANGOUT service. Smaller groups also use SKYPE. We're watching the development of BIG BLUE BUTTON, a free and open-source real-time meeting platform, as it develops the full suite of tools that are currently only available for a fee. Dozens of other free, ad-supported and/or freemium webconferencing systems such as BIG MARKER and DIM-DIM can be found in lists like HOWARD RHEINGOLD's and ROBIN GOOD's. Free phone conferencing services provide another technological "lowest common denominator": some provide a few extras like downloadable recordings.

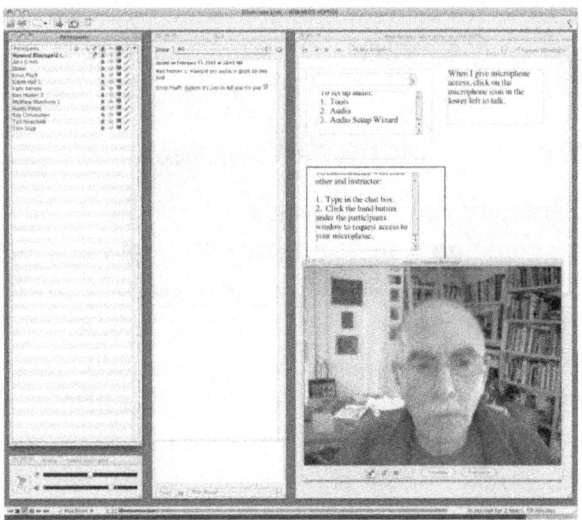

Features of real-time meeting platforms

There are many free services for chat, screen-sharing, whiteboards, and video conferencing, but combining all these components in separate panes of the same screen (preferably) or as separate tabs of a browser can have a powerful synchronizing and harmonizing effect on the group. The features to look for in meeting platforms include:

Audio and video: Choose platforms that enable voice-over-internet-protocol (VOIP) and easy ways for participants to configure their microphones and speakers. Today's webcams, together with adequate lighting and a broadband connection, enable a number of people to be visible at the same time. In Blackboard Collaborate, the person who is speaking at a given moment is visible in the largest video pane, while other participants are available in smaller video windows. Audio and video convey much more of a human dimension than text communications alone. A group of people who have seen and heard each other online are able to work together via asynchronous media such as forums and wikis more effectively. Online face-to-face meetings are often the best way for a group to argue constructively and decide on critical issues. Forums and email are comparatively bad choices for distributed decison-making.

Slide pushing: The best platforms will convert .ppt or .pdf files for sequential display. With the addition of text chat, annotations to slides, and the ability to "raise your hand" or interrupt with your voice, an online lecture can be a more multidimensional experience than even a highly discursive in-person lecture.

Text chat: As a backchannel, a means of quickly exchanging links to relevant resources, a channel for collaborative note-taking, a way of communicating with the lecturer and with other participants, text chat adds a particularly useful dimension to real-time peeragogical meetings – especially when the division of labor is explicitly agreed upon in advance. We've found that even in meetings that use the real-time collaborative editor ETHERPAD for collaborative note taking, participants may gravitate toward the built-in chat box for discussion.

Screen sharing: The ability of participants to show each other what is on their screens becomes especially important in peer learning, where we all have some things to show each other.

Web tours: An alternative to screen-sharing is the ability to display the same web page(s) to all participants by entering URLs.

Interactive whiteboards: A shared space that enables participants to enter text, drawings, shapes, colors, to move and resize media, and to import graphic content – especially if it allows anonymous actions – can foster the feeling of participating in a collective intelligence. Collaborative anonymous mind-mapping of the discussion is one technique to try with whiteboards. The whiteboard can also be used to generate an emergent agenda for an "un-meeting".

Configuring Google+ Hangout - a free alternative for up to 10 people

For up to 10 people, each equipped with a webcam, microphone, and broadband connection, GOOGLE+ HANGOUT can provide high-quality audio-video conferencing. By enabling the text-chat feature and adding Google Docs, screensharing, and SketchUp (whiteboard), it is possible to emulate most of what the commercial services offer. Adobe Connect and Blackboard Collaborate currently have the user-interface advantage of displaying chat, video, whiteboard/slides as resizable panes on one screen; at present, the free Google services can provide a powerful extension of the basic audio-video platform, but participants have to shift between different tabs or windows in the browser. Note that it is possible to STREAM A HANGOUT AND RECORD IT TO YOUTUBE, again at no cost to the user.

Suggestions for real-time meetings

In the nine online courses I have facilitated, the emphasis on co-learning encouraged participants to suggest and shape active roles during real-time meetings. By creating and taking on roles, and shifting from role to role, participants engage in a kind of collective learning about collective learning which can be as pleasurable as well as useful. Typically we first brainstorm, then analyze, then organize and present the knowledge that we discover, construct, and ultimately convey together.

Roles for participants in real-time meetings

- **Searchers:** search the web for references mentioned during the session and other resources relevant to the discussion, and publish the URLs in the text chat

- **Contextualizers:** add two or three sentences of contextual description for each URL

- **Summarizers:** note main points made through text chat.

- **Lexicographers:** identify and collaboratively define words and phrases on a wiki page.

- **Mappers:** keep track of top level and secondary level categories and help the group mindmapping exercise at the end of the session.

- **Curators:** compile the summaries, links to the lexicon and mindmaps, contextualized resources, on a single wiki page.

- **Emergent Agendas:** using the whiteboard for anonymous nomination and preference polling for agenda items, with voice, video, and text-chat channels for discussing nominations, a group can quickly set its own agenda for the real-time session.

The Paragogical Action Review

Charlie Danoff and Joe Corneli remixed the US Army's "After Action Review" to make a technique for evaluating peer learning as it happens. The five steps in the PAR are:

1. Review what was supposed to happen
2. Establish what is happening/happened
3. Determine what's right and wrong with what we are doing/have done
4. What did we learn or change?

5. What else should we change going forward?

Participants can run through these steps during live meetings to reassess the medium, the readings, the group dynamics, or any other choices that have learning relevance. The focus in the PAR is on change: as such, it provides a simple way to implement the "double loop learning" of Chris Argris (see references).

References

1. Argyris, Chris. "TEACHING SMART PEOPLE HOW TO LEARN." Harvard Business Review, 69.3, 1991.

2. Charles Jeffrey Danoff, Joseph Corneli, and Dr. Muhammed Bello Umar, THE PARAGOGICAL ACTION REVIEW, submitted to *The African Journal of Information Systems*.

Resources

- Howard Rheingold's webconferencing BOOKMARKS
- BIG BLUE BUTTON
- BLACKBOARD COLLABORATE
- GOOGLE HANGOUTS
- BIG MARKER

Part X

Resources

CHAPTER 29

HOW TO GET INVOLVED IN THE PEERAGOGY PROJECT

This page is for people who want to help develop/improve this handbook.

If you want to get involved, write to HOWARD RHEINGOLD *at* HOWARD@RHEINGOLD.COM.

Illustrations by AMANDA LYONS.

Hello and welcome!

The peeragogy project was kicked off around the time of HOWARD RHEINGOLD's January 23, 2012 REGENTS LECTURE at UC Berkeley on *Social Media and Peer Learning: From Mediated Pedagogy to Peeragogy*. We have put together a handbook about peer learning: you're reading it – maybe on OUR WEBSITE, or in your hammock with the beverage of your choice and our PRINT ON DEMAND paperback. Or maybe you grabbed our FREE PDF or some other remixed version in some other format or flavor from some other place (which would be COOL!).

But: there's still MORE WORK TO BE DONE. We created this page because you might be interested in getting involved in improving the book or furthering the project in other ways. If so, we're happy to have you aboard!

What you do here is largely up to you. Asking questions is actually extremely helpful: there's almost always someone in our GOOGLE+ COMMUNITY who would be happy to try to answer them, or refer you to someone else who can. Or email Howard and ask for a login on our Social Media Classroom, and browse through the orientation material on the SMC Wiki. Say hi in the forums. Or just poke around the public pages on peeragogy.org and leave a comment or two. Better still, find an area where you feel knowledgeable – or are willing to learn – and start writing (or filming, dancing, drawing, building, etc.).

The goal we have in mind for our book is for it be a useful guide to peer learning! To achieve that goal we have in mind multiple opportunities for peers to contribute:

- Once we get to know you a little bit we'll be happy to give you a login on peeragogy.org and you can start editing and improving this.

- You can go right ahead and post some links to relevant resources, either in comments here, or in the G+ or SMC.

- Write the text for a new sub-section (this page was once "new" – but it's been revised many times by now!).

- We're particularly interested in case studies about Peeragogy in Action!

- Organize a team to tackle a larger section or topic.

- Make a video (like these on our YouTube Channel),

- Take notes of live meetings, or grow concept maps,

- Organize a newsletter for your group or the whole team,

- Add general purpose bookmarks to THIS DIIGO GROUP, or post comments and editorial notes about peeragogy.org in THIS ONE; and

- Discuss peer learning matters and this handbook informally with us and with others!

It's up to you. Instead of worrying too much about THE RULES, join our conversations, take advantage of the digital memory of the forum to rewind the conversation all the way to the beginning (if you want to go that far), listen in for a little bit if you want to, and jump in whenever you're ready. We won't know what you're up to until you speak up. You can have a look at the outstanding tasks and teams that are listed on THIS GOOGLE DOC: our ROADMAP is a useful shared resource too. You can add to these at any time.

We regularly use Google+, Google Hangouts, forums, and email to communicate asynchronously and pretty much continuously. We also meet irregularly as a group for synchronous audio-video sessions. Further details about all these methods of communication can be found below.

In short: here's how it works:

Summary: Ways we Communicate

FORUMS AND WIKI - The project got started in the SOCIAL MEDIA CLASSROOM hosted by Howard at Howard Rheingold University. To use this resource, you'll need to contact Howard via the email address above, and he'll create a login for you. This system is asynchronous (you can participate whenever you'd like). There are lots of old conversations in the forums that you can read to see how the community of peeragogy handbook creators formed – and you can add your own voice. You'll find extended discussions of issues and decisions raised in live sessions.

GOOGLE+ COMMUNITY - We created the "Peeragogy in Action" community as a place to gather stories about how people are applying peeragogy techniques. We're also using it to coordinate work on the Peeragogy Project itself. Feel free to JOIN US!

LIVE SESSIONS - We meet synchronously at agreed-upon times, using audio, video, text chat, slides, screen-sharing. For groups of ten or more, we use Blackboard Collaborate, for which Howard has a 50-seat-at-a-time license. These sessions are recorded. For information about scheduling, and recordings, see THE FORUM TOPIC. Participation requires a fairly fast (broadband) Internet connection, a microphone or headset, and (if you wish), a webcam. For groups of ten or smaller (usually for project teams), we use Google+ Hangouts. Individual teams do their own scheduling.

TWITTER LIST - Follow @PEERAGOGY & to get added to the Peeragogy Twitter list please post your Twitter name HERE. Stephanie Schipper will then add you.

TWITTER HASHTAG: #PEERAGOGY We even have a FACEBOOK PAGE.

Questions?

If you have questions, that's good! Use Google+ or the forums, post a comment on this page, email the team energy center if you know who that is, or email HOWARD@RHEINGOLD.COM.

CHAPTER 30

PEERAGOGY IN ACTION

We have been writing the missing manual for peer-produced peer learning - the "Peeragogy Handbook" (PEERAGOGY.ORG). Throughout the building of this work, we, ourselves peer learners in this quest, have been mindful of these four questions:

1. *How does a motivated group of self-learners choose a subject or skill to learn?*

2. *How can this group identify and select the best learning resources about that topic?*

3. *How will these learners identify and select the appropriate technology and communications tools and platforms to accomplish their learning goal?*

4. *What does the group need to know about learning theory and practice to put together a successful peer-learning program?*

It is clear to us that the techniques of peer production that have built and continue to improve *Wikipedia* and GNU/Linux have yet to fully demonstrate their power in education. We believe that the *Peeragogy Handbook* can help change that by building a distributed community of peer learners/educators, and a strongly vetted collection of best practices. Our project complements others' work on sites like Wikiversity and P2PU, and builds upon understandings that have developed informally in distributed communities of hobbyists and professionals, as well as in (and beyond) the classrooms of generations of passionate educators. Here, we present Peeragogy in Action, a project guide in four parts. Each part relates to one or more sections of our handbook, and suggests activities to try while you explore peer learning. These activities are designed for flexible use by widely distributed groups, collaborating via a light-weight infrastructure. Participants may be educators, community organizers, designers, hackers, dancers, students, seasoned peeragogues, or first-timers. The guide should be useful for groups who want to build a strong collaboration, as well as to facilitators or theorists who want to hone their practice or approach. Together, we will use our various talents to build effective methods and models for peer produced peer learning. Let's get started!

Setting the initial challenge and building a framework for accountability among participants is an important starting point.

Activity – Come up with a plan for your work and an agreement, or informal contract, for your group. You can use the suggestions in this guide as a starting point, but your first task is to revise the plan to suit your needs. It might be helpful to ask: What are you interested in learning? What is your primary intended outcome? What problem do you hope to solve? How collaborative does your project need to be? How will the participants' expertise in the topic vary? What sort of support will you and other participants require? What problems won't you solve?

Technology – Familiarize yourself with the collaboration tools you intend to use (e.g. Wordpress, Git and LaTeX, YouTube, GIMP, a public wiki, a private forum, or something else) and create a first post, edit, or video introducing yourself and your project(s) to others in the worldwide peeragogy community.

Suggested Resources – The Peeragogy Handbook, parts I ('INTRODUCTION') and II ('PEER LEARNING'). You may also want to work through a short lesson called IMPLEMENTING PARAGOGY, from the early days before the Peeragogy project was convened. For a succinct theoretical treatment, please refer to our literature review, which we have adapted into a WIKIPEDIA PAGE.

Further Reading – Boud, D. and Lee, A. (2005). *'Peer learning' as pedagogic discourse for research education.* Studies in Higher Education, 30(5):501–516.

Observations from the Peeragogy project – We had a fairly weak project structure at the outset, which yielded mixed results. One participant said: "I definitely think I do better when presented with a framework or scaffold to use for participation or content development." Yet the same person wrote with enthusiasm about models of entrepreneurship, saying she was "freed of the requirement or need for an entrepreneurial visionary." In short,

Other people can support you in achieving your goal and make the work more fun too.

Activity – Write an invitation to someone who can help as a co-facilitator on your project. Clarify what you hope to learn from them and what your project has to offer. Helpful questions to consider: What resources are available or missing? What do you already have that you can build on? How will you find the necessary resources? Who else is interested in these kinds of challenges? The two of you should be able to come up with a respectable list.

Technology – Identify tools that could potentially be useful during the project, even if it's new to you. Start learning how to use them. Connect with people in other locales who share similar interests or know the tools.

Suggested resources – The Peeragogy Handbook, parts III ('CONVENING A GROUP') and IV ('ORGANIZING A LEARNING CONTEXT').

Recommended Reading – Schmidt, J. Philipp. (2009). Commons-Based Peer Production and education. Free Culture Research Workshop Harvard University, 23 October 2009.

Observations from the Peeragogy project – We used a strategy of "open enrollment." New people were welcome to join the project at any time. We also encouraged people to either stay involved or withdraw; several times over the past year, we required participants to explicitly reaffirm interest in order to stay registered in the forum and mailing list. This choice cut down on the distraction of wondering if inactive members would reconnect. Still, the project continued to accumulate content, which gave some newcomers the discouraging feeling that there was too much to catch up on. Those who ended up being the most productive dove right in and didn't worry about making mistakes. The most active members were gracious and patient with the newcomers - an important quality in successful peer-learning facilitators.

Solidifying your work plan and learning strategy together with concrete measures for 'success' can move the project forward significantly. Working in teams and sharing information with others will help you to develop your project.

Activity – Distill your ideas by writing an essay, making visual sketches, or creating a short video to communicate the unique plans for organization and evaluation that your group will use. By this time, you should have identified which aspects of the project need to be refined or expanded. Dive in!

Technology – Take time to mentor others or be mentored by someone, meeting up in person or online. Pair up with someone else and share knowledge together about one or more tools. You can discuss some of the difficulties that you've encountered, or teach a beginner some tricks.

Suggested resources – The Peeragogy Handbook, parts V ('Co-facilitation and Co-working'), VI ('Assessment'), and part VII ('Patterns, Use cases, and Examples').

Recommended reading – Argyris, Chris. "Teaching smart people how to learn." Harvard Business Review 69.3 (1991); and, Gersick, Connie J.G. "Time and transition in work teams: Toward a new model of group development." Academy of Management Journal 31.1 (1988): 9-41.

Observations from the Peeragogy project – Perhaps one of the most important roles in the Peeragogy project was the role of the 'Wrapper', who prepared and circulated weekly summaries of forum activity. This helped people stay informed about what was happening in the project even if they didn't have time to read the forums. We've also found that small groups of people who arrange their own meetings are often the most productive.

Wrap up the project with a critical assessment of progress and directions for future work. Share any changes to this syllabus that you think would be useful for future peeragogues!

Activity – Identify the main obstacles you encountered. What are some goals you were not able to accomplish yet? Did you foresee these challenges at the outset? How did this project resemble or differ from others you've worked on? How would you do things differently in future projects? What would you like to tackle next?

Writing – Communicate your reflection case. Prepare a short written or multimedia essay, dealing with your experiences in this course. Share the results by posting it where others in the broader Peeragogy project can find it.

'Extra credit' – Contribute back to one of the other organisations or projects that helped you on this peeragogical journey. Think about what you have to offer. Is it a bug fix, a constructive critique, pictures, translation help, PR, wiki-gnoming or making a cake? Make it something special, and people will remember you and thank you for it.

Suggested resources – The Peeragogy Handbook, parts VIII ('Technologies, Services, and Platforms') and IX ('Resources').

Recommended reading – Stallman, Richard. "Why software should be free" (1992).

Peeragogy in Action

Observations from the Peeragogy project – When we were deciding how to license our work, various Creative Commons licences were proposed (CC Zero, CC By-SA and CC By-SA-NC). After a brief discussion, no one was in favor of restricting downstream users, so we decided to use CC0. In connection with this discussion, we agreed that we would work on ways to explicitly build 're-usability' into the handbook content.

Micro-Case Study: The Peeragogy Project, Year 1

Since its conception in early 2012, the Peeragogy Project has collected over 3700 comments in our discussion forum, and over 200 pages of expository text in the handbook. It has given contributors a new way of thinking about things together. However, the project has not had the levels of engagement that should be possible, given the technology available, the global interest in improving education, and the number of thoughtful participants who expressed interest. We hope that the handbook and this accompanying syllabus will provide a seed for a new phase of learning, with many new contributors and new ideas drawn from real-life applications.

CHAPTER 31

STYLE GUIDE

Format your HTML nicely

We need to be able to process the content from this Wordpress site and turn it into various formats like LaTeX and EPUB. Our automated tools work much better if pages are formatted with simple and uniform HTML markup. Some key points:

- Mark up your links: use THE PEERAGOGY HANDBOOK instead of HTTP://PEERAGOGY.ORG. It's best if the link text is somewhat descriptive.

- Use a numbered list to format your references (see CONVENING A GROUP for one example of an article that gets this right!)

- Wordpress does not automatically add paragraph tags to your paragraphs. If you want your text to appear justified and if you want the paragraphs to transfer to downstream formats, switch to HTML editing mode and wrap individual paragraphs with `<p style="text-align: justify;">...</p>`

- Use Heading 2 and Heading 3 tags to mark up sections, not **bold** text. If you use bold or italics in your paragraphs, you should **check** that the markup *is actually correct*. It should exactly surround the words that you're marking up – `<em>like this</em>` – and it should not include extra spaces around marked up words – `<em> NOT like this </em>`.

Keep it short

The easiest sections to read are those that are shorter and include some kind of visual (video or image) and have some personal connection (i.e. they tell a story). For anything longer, break it up into sub-pages, add visuals, make sure each sub-page is accessible to someone (who is it?). Think clearly of this reader, talk to them.

Make it clear

We'll illustrate this point by example. The original full title of the book was "The Peeragogy Handbook: A resource for self-organizing self-learners". But "SELF-ORGANIZING" is a technical term, and "self-learner" is a confusing neologism. We shouldn't use technical terms unless we explain them. So we really shouldn't use it in the first sentence or paragraph, or title, of the book because we'll scare people off or confuse them. If we want to explain what "self-organization" means and why it is relevant for peeragogy, then we can take a chapter to do that much later on in the book. At the same time, we shouldn't try to "say the same thing in a simpler way." We should try to get rid of the technical concept completely and see what's left. The easiest thing to do in such cases is to delete the sentence completely and start over: when in doubt, speak plainly.

Don't overdo it with bullet points

Maybe this is just a "pet peeve", but I find text very hard to read when there are more than a few bullet points included. For me, it works better when the bullet points are replaced with numbered lists (which should still be used sparingly). It also seems that when many disjointed bullet points appear, sometimes the author is really just indexing the main points that are presented better in someone else's narrative. Therefor, consider replacing an entire bulleted list with a reference to someone else's book/webpage/chapter. In today's hyperlinked world, it's easy enough for the reader to go elsewhere to get good content (and indeed, we should make it easy for them to find the best treatments around!). In particular, it is not entirely pleasant to *read* a taxonomy. Maybe that sort of thing can be moved into an appendix if we need to have it.

Include activities

In today's live meeting, we agreed that activities would not magically solve all possible usability/readability problems, but they are good to have anyway. And, according to our page layout, each chapter should have at least one activity (linked to from the sidebar). So, when reading the book, please make note of any activity that can be included. (Also make note of problems that *won't* be solved by adding activities!)

Don't be overly chatty

In our efforts to escape from academia-speak and simplify the text in the handbook, it's important to make sure we are not heading towards the other extreme – being too conversational. When we're having a conversation with someone, we tend to pepper our ideas with transitional or pivotal phrases ("In any event," "With that said," "As I mentioned elsewhere," etc.) that help to keep the talk flowing. We also go off on brief tangents before making our way back to the main topic, and sometimes express ourselves in run-on sentences. While this is perfectly natural in speech, it can be confusing and complex when being read (in our handbook or elsewhere). Let's stay conscious of our audience and try to meet that perfect balance of simple, yet professional in our writing.

Additional style bonus points

- Avoid double spaces after paragraphs; this is a leftover from the age of typewriters and can create "rivers" of white space.

Style Guide

- Capitalize the first word of each item in a bulleted list, especially if items include a verb form (this list and the one above are examples!).
- Capitalize the first word of headings and subheadings; lower case all others.

CHAPTER 32

MEET THE AUTHORS

Bryan Alexander — USA, VT (Author) I research the ways new technologies change education, teaching, learning, and scholarship. I'm passionate about storytelling, gaming, pedagogy, and understanding the future. My family homesteads on top of a little mountain, raising food. BRYAN ON TWITTER | BRYAN'S PERSONAL WEBSITE

Paul Allison — USA, NY (Author) Currently, I teach English at the BRONX ACADEMY SENIOR HIGH. Another community that I'm a part of is the NEW YORK CITY WRITING PROJECT. I'm the NYC Technology Liaison for the NATIONAL WRITING PROJECT. I help to manage YOUTH VOICES and I co-produce TEACHERS TEACHING TEACHERS. PAUL ON GOOGLE+ | PAUL'S PERSONAL WEBSITE

Meet the Authors

María F. Arenas — República Argentina (Author, Editor) Independent consultant researcher on TICS applied to Learning, Digital Communication, Institutional, Corporate. On line facilitator tutorship. Professor on Semiotics, Social Communication, Networking. MARÍA ON GOOGLE+ | MARÍA'S PERSONAL WEBSITE

Régis Barondeau — Canada (Author) I build bridges between research, praxeology and technology and I become creative "by finding a likeness between things which were not thought alike before" (Bronowski, 1958). I'm interested in complexity, culture, social media especially wikis, education, open government and more. Reach RÉGIS ON TWITTER | REGIS' PERSONAL WEBSITE

Doug Breitbart — USA, NJ (Author, Meeting Support) I a catalyst and provocateur who has worn the hats of attorney, consultant, facilitator, coach, entrepreneur, father, husband, student, teacher. DOUG ON LINKEDIN | DOUG'S PERSONAL WEBSITE

Meet the Authors

George Brett — USA, VAN (Author, Edior, Meeting Support) Twitter Bio: "autodidactic techno arsty craftsy eclecticist." Many years as a diplomat for IT technology as applied to research and education. I'm a teacher/trainer, consultant, analyst, info ferret, artist, life-long learner, and member of a great family. Current challenges include: best way to share skills and experiences with others and as a Gen-Boomer finding more steady work. GEORGE ON LINKEDIN | GEORGE'S PERSONAL WEBSITE

Suz Burroughs - USA, CA (Author, Designer) I enable the connections between the teacher and learner in all of us by designing robust, measurable learning environments where people share their knowledge and experience with each other. Learning Designer, Design Thinking facilitator, Visiting Professor of Innovation. SUZ' PERSONAL WEBSITE

Meet the Authors

Joe Corneli — U.K. (Author, Editor) Joe Corneli does research on the anthropology of modern mathematics. He is a member of the board of directors of the US-based nonprofit, PlanetMath.org, and a research student at the Knowledge Media Institute of The Open University, UK. Reach JOE ON IDENTI.CA | JOE'S PERSONAL WEBSITE

Jay Cross — USA, CA (Author) Jay is the Johnny Appleseed of informal learning. The INTERNET TIME ALLIANCE, which he chairs, helps corporations and governments use networks to accelerate performance. JAY BY EMAIL | JAY'S PERSONAL WEBSITE

Charles Jeffrey Danoff — USA, IL (Author) Charles is the Owner of Mr. Danoff's Teaching Laboratory, an Educational Publishing and Services firm he established in 2009. He started co-publishing research on Paragogy, Peeragogy's inspiration, in late 2010. CHARLES ON IDENTI.CA | CHARLES' PERSONAL WEBSITE

Meet the Authors

James Folkestad - USA, CO (Author, Editor, Designer, Developer) My approach to education has shifted from an emphasis on my teaching, to a more central focus on student learning, and finally to an activity-systems approach as I have come to realize that the two (teacher and learner) are inseparable parts of the learning ecosystem. Reach JAMES ON GOOGLE+ | JAMES' PERSONAL WEBSITE

John Graves - Australia (Editor) Founder of SlideSpeech. Graduate of Singularity University.

Reach JOHN ON TWITTER | JOHN'S PERSONAL WEBSITE

Gigi Johnson, EdD — USA, CA (Author, Developer) I mix formal learning programs with programs to help learners begin to work, live, and create everywhere. My own adventures include writing, singing, video, teaching, and parenting 3 teens. GIGI ON TWITTER | GIGI'S PERSONAL PAGE

Meet the Authors

Anna Keune — Germany/Finland (Co-author, Designer) I design technology for learning and I like it. I'm affiliated with the Media Lab Helsinki, Aalto University School of Arts, Design and Architecture. ANNA ON TWITTER | ANNA'S PERSONAL WEBSITE

Kyle Larson — FL, USA (Editor) Kyle Larson is an undergraduate thesis student at New College of Florida. His research interests include composition theory, rhetorical theory, computers and composition, and pedagogy. KYLE ON GOOGLE+

Roland Legrand — Belgium (Author) I'm a financial journalist, heavily involved in experimenting with social media and new forms for reporting and community conversation. ROLAND ON TWITTER | ROLAND'S PERSONAL WEBSITE

Meet the Authors

Amanda Lyons — USA, NY DesignerI am a Visual Practitioner, Organization Development Consultant & Experiential Educator. I love helping people communicate via visual tools that generally include markers and paper. I think our education system could benefit from using visual communication tools as well as text based methods. Reach AMANDA ON TWITTER | AMANDA'S PERSONAL WEBSITE

Christopher Neal — USA, WA (Communications and Media) I am driven by technology and its ability to modify virtual communities and social media, and a passion for Social:Learn, Social:iA, Situated Cognition, Social Learning Theory, Connectivism, etc. CHRISTOPHER ON GOOGLE+ | CHRISTOPHER'S PERSONAL WEBSITE

Ted Newcomb — USA, AZ (Author, Project Management) Happily retired grandpa, curating on digital culture, sociology of the web; interested in collaboration and cooperation in digital networks that result in positive change. TED ON ABOUT.ME | TED'S PERSONAL WEBSITE

Meet the Authors

Howard Rheingold — USA, CA (Author, Editor) Inspired by Charles Danoff and Joe Corneli's work on paragogy, I instigated the Peeragogy project in order to provide a resource for self-organizing self-learners. Learning is my passion. Reach HOWARD ON TWITTER | HOWARD'S PERSONAL WEBSITE

Paola Ricaurte — Mexico (Author) My believe: education and technology are essential tools for social change. My challenges: activist, teacher, mother, immigrant. My philosophy: I am what I am because of who we all are. PAOLA ON TWITTER | PAOLA'S PERSONAL WEBSITE

Fabrizio Terzi — Italy (Inventor, Designer, Translator) I am involved in social and educational projects related to public access to knowledge and cultural diversity. I am an active member of FSF and the FTG – working on Free Culture. FABRIZIO ON IDENTICA | FABRIZIO'S PERSONAL WEBSITE

Geoff Walker — U.K. (Author) A Further and Higher Education Lecturer and Tutor, social networker, e-learning advocate. GEOFF ON TWITTER | GEOFF'S PERSONAL WEBSITE

These materials are made available under the terms of CREATIVE COMMONS 0 COPYRIGHT WAIVER instead of a "traditional" copyleft license. We the undersigned agree to the following, wherein "this work" refers to "The Peeragogy Handbook" and all other content posted on PEERAGOGY.ORG or the original collaboratory site, HTTP://SOCIALMEDIACLASSROOM.COM/HOST/PEERAGOGY.

I hereby waive all copyright and related or neighboring rights together with all associated claims and causes of action with respect to this work to the extent possible under the law.

Signed:

- Bryan Alexander
- Paul Allison
- Régis Barondeau
- Doug Breitbart
- George Brett
- Suz Burroughs
- Joseph Corneli
- Jay Cross
- Charles Jeffrey Danoff
- Julian Elve
- María Fernanda
- James Folkestad
- Kathy Gill
- John Graves

Meet the Authors

- Gigi Johnson
- Anna Keune
- Kyle Larson
- Roland Legrand
- Amanda Lyons
- Christopher Tillman Neal
- Ted Newcomb
- Stephanie Parker
- Charlotte Pierce
- David Preston
- Howard Rheingold
- Paola Ricaurte
- Verena Roberts
- Stephanie Schipper
- Fabrizio Terzi
- Geoff Walker

Note that this waiver does not apply to other works by the above authors, including works linked to from PEERAGOGY.ORG. It also does not apply to embedded content drawn from other sites and included for the reader's convenience.

Future contributors: Note also that we will require a similar copyright waiver agreement. That said, the waiver also means that you are free to do essentially whatever you like with the content in your own work! Have fun!

How we came to this decision

These Creative Commons license options were proposed by various members of the community:

- *CC Zero* - public domain; no restrictions for downstream users
- *CC By-SA* - requires downstream users to include attribution and to license their work in the same way
- *CC By-SA-NC* - requires downstream users to include attribution, to license their work in the same way and disallows any commercial use of the content

After a brief discussion, no one was in favor of restricting downstream users, so we decided to go with CC0. We agreed that we would get enough "credit" by having our names on PEERAGOGY.ORG. In connection with this discussion, we agreed that we would work on ways to explicitly build "reusability" into the handbook content.

www.ingramcontent.com/pod-product-compliance
Lightning Source LLC
Chambersburg PA
CBHW022354040426
42450CB00005B/184